Designer Scrapbooks

with

ANNA
GRIFFIN

Memorable Moments Captured with Style

Designer Scrapbooks

with

ANNA GRIFFIN

Memorable Moments Captured with Style

Sterling Publishing Co. New York
A Sterling/Chapelle Book

Chapelle, Ltd.: Jo Packham, Sara Toliver, Cindy Stoeckl

Editor: Lana Hall

Art Director: Karla Haberstich

Graphic Illustrator: Kim Taylor

Copy Editor: Marilyn Goff

Staff: Kelly Ashkettle, Areta Bingham, Donna Chambers, Emily Frandsen, Mackenzie Johnson, Susan Jorgensen, Jennifer Luman, Melissa Maynard, Barbara Milburn, Lecia Monsen, Suzy Skadburg, Kim Taylor, Linda Venditti, Desirée Wybrow

Anna Griffin, Inc.: Anna Griffin, Tracey Chabot Flammer

Art Director: Holley Silirie

Scrapbook Page Contributors: Jenna Beegle, Tracey Chabot Flammer, Debby Schuh, Holley Silirie

Photography: Chris Little Photography;
　　　　　　 Ryne Hazen, Kevin Dilley, at Hazen Photography

If you have any questions or comments, please contact:
Chapelle, Ltd., Inc., P.O. Box 9252, Ogden, UT 84409
(801) 621-2777 • (801) 621-2788 Fax
e-mail: chapelle@chapelleltd.com
web site: www.chapelleltd.com

　　　Library of Congress Cataloging-in-Publication Data
Griffin, Anna.
　Designer scrapbooks with Anna Griffin : memorable moments captured with
　style / Anna Griffin.
　　　p. cm.
　"A Sterling/Chapelle Book."
　ISBN 1-4027-1029-1
　1. Photograph albums. 2. Photographs--Conservation and restoration.
　3. Scrapbooks. I. Title.
　TR465 .G76 2004
　745.593--dc22

　　　　　　　　　2003023620

10 9 8 7 6 5 4 3 2 1

Published by Sterling Publishing Co., Inc.
387 Park Avenue South, New York, NY 10016
©2004 by Anna Griffin
Distributed in Canada by Sterling Publishing
c/o Canadian Manda Group, One Atlantic Avenue, Suite 105
Toronto, Ontario, Canada M6K 3E7
Distributed in Great Britain by Chrysalis Books Group PLC
The Chrysalis Building, Bramley Road, London W10 6 SP, England
Distributed in Australia by Capricorn Link (Australia) Pty. Ltd.
P. O. Box 704, Windsor, NSW 2756, Australia
Printed in the U. S. A.
All Rights Reserved

Sterling ISBN 1-4027-1029-1

Introduction

Inspired by the traditions that I cherish from my family and the stories that I have heard from many scrapbook enthusiasts, I set out to create a book that would help to give you memorable moments with your family, as well as create elegant scrapbooks to preserve those memories.

There are many levels of inspiration in this book. First, I encourage you to create new traditions within your family. Then, I give you ways to commemorate these family traditions on scrapbook pages year after year. Each layout has a unique technique or embellishment, a color palette, and a pattern you can use as your own. I hope you have as much fun making these pages as I did.

Table of Contents

ANNA GRIFFIN

Invitation Design

Beginnings

There is nothing

more powerful

than an idea

whose time has come.

- Victor Hugo

This quote is pinned to the bulletin board in my office, which is pictured on page 6. It inspires me to create with each new day.

One of the first questions people always ask me is how I got started, so here goes. I grew up in my great-grandmother's house surrounded with all of my great-grandmother's antique things in a tiny town outside of Charlotte, North Carolina, called Marshville. I always dreamed of having my own business; and it is no surprise considering that my family is full of artists and entrepreneurs.

I was very fortunate to be raised in an environment where I was encouraged and taught that anything is possible. I credit my ever-so-elegant grandmother with igniting my passion for antiques and beautiful things which are the cornerstone of my business today.

With a degree in Environmental Design from North Carolina State University, my career as a graphic designer has taken me from Atlanta to New York and back. I worked as an art director in a design firm, a marketing director for a software company, and even a salesperson for renowned designer Vera Wang before starting my own custom wedding invitation business in 1995. The original designs and attention to detail filled a void in the wedding industry by offering a much needed, high-quality alternative to the traditional engraved invitation.

In 1996, the business expanded to include a wholesale division that offered imprintable invitations with a custom look. Brides were now able to purchase a box of invitations from a local stationery store, print them at home and have the result be as elegant as a custom designed product. My signature vellum and ribbon, combined with the use of antique engravings, botanicals, and fabrics, were truly special and began a trend that is still popular in the industry today.

The line was an immediate success and although it has expanded to include many products, the design philosophy remains constant. I want people to look at my products and experience beauty. I want someone to receive my invitations and feel they've received a gift.

The product line expanded in 1998 to include elegant note cards, notepads, and greeting cards. These lovely papers quickly became a favorite with upscale gift stores, garden shops and antique stores. In 2001, the line grew to include home office products. Beautiful file folders, mailing labels, office pads, and letterhead were designed to decorate work spaces, either at home or at the office.

I was very fortunate to be raised in an environment where I was encouraged and taught that anything is possible.

With the growing trend in the workforce to work out of one's home, I saw the need for beautiful desk accessories to enhance one's personal work space. Photo albums and guest books, address books and journals featuring hand-tied ribbons round out this delightful collection.

Also in 2001, I entered the craft industry with the Anna Griffin Decorative Papers line, consisting of the beautiful papers, frames, and albums you will see used in this book. Designed exclusively for the more discerning scrapbook creator, the line fills a void in the craft industry by offering consumers beautiful, high-quality papers with a uniqueness all their own. The colorful botanical images coordinate with solids, stripes, and tone-on-tone patterns to create beautiful pages.

The products also include antique die-cut frames, Victorian die-cuts, journaling pages, elegant satin ribbons, and scrapbook albums. It was a natural progression for the company as my archives of images easily lend themselves to this new category.

What inspires me in design are luxurious patterns, antique textiles, and rich floral prints.

My designs are a reflection of my passion for antiques, prints, and fine textiles. The antique botanicals can be found on the walls of my home, while the collection of French fabrics are images taken from flea markets all over the world. What motivates me in design are luxurious patterns, antique textiles and rich floral prints. Simple and elegant!

I have enjoyed enormous success in the last eight years. My products have been featured in many national magazines such as *Victoria*, *Martha Stewart Living*, and *Better Homes and Gardens*. You can find our things in fine retail stores worldwide. Thanks to you, the demand for our products continues to grow.

The second question people always ask me is "What's next?" The answer is always that anything is possible!

Scrapbook

TRADITIONS

There are no days in life so memorable as those
which vibrated to some stroke of the imagination.

Ralph Waldo Emerson

Scrapbook pages are traditionally made from photos of events
that have occurred in the past. What if you started traditions today
especially for the scrapbook pages you will create tomorrow?
What I mean is, starting a tradition of taking the same kind of
photograph year after year, and making an entire scrapbook about it.
This book tells the story of wonderful family traditions that are
meant to inspire your scrapbooks for years to come.

Readers will find photographs and instructions on how to make
each scrapbook page, following each chapter. Templates supporting
each project, if suggested, will be found in the final section of the book.
In the materials lists, papers, motifs, and die-cuts are suggestions.
If the exact Anna Griffin products are desired, refer to the catalog
numbers indicated in parentheses after the item's description.

© ANNA GRIFFIN INC.
AG341 · MADE IN USA
LIGNIN FREE · ACID FREE

Birthday
TRADITIONS

Sing a song of birthdays, full of fun and cheer,
and may you keep on having them,
for many a happy year.

- Anonymous

My fondest memories of childhood center around my birthday.
This is because my mother always found a way to make that day
the most special of the entire year. I got to be "queen for the day,"
eat whatever I wanted, and even have one wish granted.
While my elaborate birthday cakes only lasted a matter of minutes,
the following scrapbook pages commemorate those
memories for the rest of my life.

My First
Birthday CAKE

August 5, 1967

Birthday Cake

A BIRTHDAY TRADITION

Chocolate, vanilla, and strawberry were my favorite kinds of cakes as a child. Give me a corner piece with at least one rose and lots of icing and I was in heaven. Those days are over, and now the only place I can have all of that icing is in my scrapbook!

SUGAR & SPICE AND EVERYTHING NICE!

I GOT A BIKE!

Chocolate Cake

My 7th birthday marks the beginning
of my love for chocolate! Now, I believe
if dessert is not made of chocolate,
then it's just not dessert. Roses and
leaves made from folded paper
look just like the ones on my cake.
Roll paper to look like candles and give
them a little fire by fringing the ends.

MISSY, STEPHEN & ME

MY 7TH BIRTHDAY
AUGUST 5, 1973

Strawberry Cake

My favorite cake as a child was strawberry. My mother always made one especially for me. Re-create your favorite birthday cake in paper and frost it with decorative edges and die-cut flowers. It's just as pretty as the real thing, but without the calories!

My First *Birthday* Cake
August 5, 1967

Three-layered Cake

My childhood birthday parties were great fun because they were right before we started back to school, so everyone came! You can make your own layer cake to showcase multiple party pictures. By building each layer with dimensional tape, you will get the effect of a multitiered confection.

Happy Birthday to Me!

Birthday Wishes

A BIRTHDAY TRADITION

In my family, a birthday was a time when your wishes always came true. It seems that as the number of candles on my cake grew from year to year, so did my birthday wishes. Remember whatever you were wishing for each year by recording it in your scrapbook.

Wishes in the Wind

ON MY OWN

WISHED FOR A ROOM OF MY OWN

TH BIRTHDAY I WISH'D FOR A PUPP

WISHED FOR A NEW PARTY DRESS

SHED FOR A RECORD PLAYER

Pinwheel Wishes

Close your eyes, make a wish and blow on the pinwheel to make it come true. Just like blowing out the candles on your cake, this great paper technique can be used for favors and even to decorate your scrapbook.

SALLIE THOMPSON
12 YEARS OLD
SEPTEMBER 2, 1950

On My 23rd Birthday

Wishing for the World!

August 5, 1989

I wish for

I wish for

Secret Wishes

I believe that you have to keep your birthday wishes a secret in order for them to come true. Make miniature envelopes to keep your wishes safe this year.

This year I wish for....

A CAR

This year I wish for....

MY FIRST K

"Happy "Sweet 16" Anne

BIG WISHES ON MY 16TH BIRTHDAY
August 5, 1982

ar I w

Sweet Sixteen

Record, then conceal your
birthday wishes in a small
envelope each year. Tuck them
away in your scrapbook and reveal
them the following year. You will
be surprised how many of
them came true.

Capture the Moment

A BIRTHDAY TRADITION

My friend Tracey's mother marked
the occasion of Tracey's birthday by
taking her picture every year at the time
she was born. It just so happened that
the time was 4:25 AM and Tracey was
always asleep. What funny photos!
This is a great tradition to build upon
in your birthday scrapbook.

The day was
celebrated at the
hospital in
Charlotte, NC

I WAS

BORN AT

7:02

August 6, 1966
My first day of life

Time of Birth

Time stood still for my parents in those first few minutes after my birth. Things really haven't been the same for them since. What better way to remember the time than with an array of clip-art clock embellishments.

Sallie's Sixteenth Birthday
September 2, 1956

Birthday Presents

My mother has spent her birthday
at the beach since she was young
and still does it today. I "wrapped up"
her favorite beach memories as
presents, so she can open them
time and again.

ANNA GRIFFIN HERALDS HER 37TH YEAR!

August 5, 2003
Atlanta, Georgia
Today I celebrated my 37th birthday, surrounded by my friends and family!

Birthday Celebration:
Drinks at Twist, dinner at Blue Pointe, followed by birthday cake and gifts!

Birthday Cake:
Chocolate Oblivion Cake

Birthday Gifts:
Bathrobe and slippers from Missy, Darren and Charles; Palm Pilot from Dad; Digital camera from Mom; Bouquet of Flowers from Granny.

Birthday Feelings:
I am happy to be celebrating with my friends and family. My 36th year was great, and I'm looking forward to an even better year ahead!

Where I Lived This Year:
Peachtree Battle Avenue in Atlanta although I am moving in just a few days to my new home on West Wesley Avenue.

My Accomplishments:
• Two's Company Releases Anna Griffin Home Office Furnishings
• Anna Griffin Inc. Publishes Three New Crafting Books
• QVC Debuts Hour-Long Craft Show, Elegant Paper Crafting with Anna Griffin
• Plaid develops my silk ribbon designs.

Favorite Movie:
How to Lose a Guy in 10 Days

My 36th year was great, and I'm looking forward to an even better year ahead!

Favorite TV Shows:
The Bachelor, American Idol, Restore America and Elegant Paper Crafting with Anna Griffin

Favorite Books:
The Devil Wears Prada by Lauren Weisberger, Power Vs. Force by David Hawkins, and Shopaolic Series by Sophie Kinsella.

Places Visited This Year:
Anaheim, CA; Brazil, Chattanooga, TN; Chicago, IL; Dallas TX; London, England; New York, NY; Orlando, FL; Pittsburgh, PA.

Favorite Memories:
CKU Orlando with Tracey, shopping in London with Holley, my trip to Brazil and times spent with my nephew, Charles.

The Year Ahead:
I hope the year ahead brings fame, fortune and good health!

Happy Birthday

Newspaper Headlines

These days, life seems so hectic that I can't remember things like I used to. On my birthday, I copied my favorite section (horoscope) of the newspaper and chronicled world events in my journaling for this year's scrapbook tribute.

Birthday
TRADITIONS

BIRTHDAY CAKE
Chocolate Cake

Materials
1 sheet of Beige Solid (AG113)
1 sheet of Gold Pattern (AG027)
1 sheet of Gold Solid (AG029)
1 sheet of Green Pattern (AG003)
1 sheet of Green Stripe (AG140)
1 sheet of Pink Pattern (AG137)
1 sheet of Pink Stripe (AG086)
1 sheet of Yellow Solid (AG122)
2 sheets of Pink/Brown
    Floral (AG108)
Border punch
Cream ink pad
Decorative scissors: mini scallop
Greenery rosettes
Rubber stamp: swirl background

Directions

Using the cream ink pad, stamp a pattern on the beige solid paper with a rubber stamp. Use the Chocolate Cake templates on page 131 to make the cake and the slice with gold pattern paper and the beige stamped paper.

To make the frosting, cut several ½" strips of green pattern paper with decorative scissors. Using a craft knife, make small ¼" vertical cuts every 1" across the green strips. Cut several ³⁄₁₆" strips from the pink stripe paper. Feed the pink strips through the slits in the green strips. Pull the pink strips tighter and gather the green strips to form the border. Add pink rosettes to the bottom row of frosting.

Use a border punch on pink pattern paper to make the cake plates and photo frames, then mount to gold solid paper.

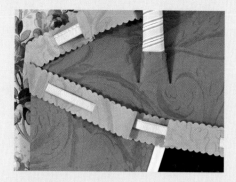

To make the candles, wrap a 3" piece of scrap paper around a pencil and secure with tape to make a tube. Then, apply double-sided adhesive to the back. Cut several ¼" strips from green stripe paper.

Wrap the ¼" strip around the tube on a diagonal. Slide off the pencil and trim to form the candle. Tightly roll a 1½" strip of yellow solid paper and insert in the top of the candle. Using scissors, make small cuts to fringe the yellow flame. Wrap base of candle with gold pattern paper, then make slits in the cake to insert candles.

Strawberry Cake

Materials
1 sheet of Bright Pink Pattern (AG085)
1 sheet of Green Pattern (AG003)
1 sheet of Pink Floral (AG101)
1 sheet of Pink Pattern (AG013)
1 sheet of Pink Pattern (AG087)
1 sheet of Pink Pattern (AG128)
1 sheet of Pink Stripe (AG086)
4 small cream buttons
Decorative paper clip

Directions
Create a border on the pink pattern paper, using four ½" strips of pink pattern paper. From the pink stripe paper cut four ¼" strips, layer and add buttons in the corners.

Using a sheet of pink pattern paper and a sheet of bright pink pattern paper, cut frosting, using the Strawberry Cake templates on page 131. Attach frosting to a different pink pattern sheet and form cake. Trim away excess paper to shape the cake.

Using a craft knife, trim flower clusters from the pink floral paper and attach to the cake. Attach photo and journaling with a decorative paper clip.

Three-layered Cake

Materials
1 sheet of Floral (AG124)
1 sheet of Pink Solid (AG015)
1 sheet of Pink Stripe (AG086)
2 sheets of Purple Pattern (AG139)
2 sheets of Yellow Pattern (AG123)
3 frames (AG418)
Decorative scissors: scallop,
  wide scallop, wide seagull

Directions
Trim the floral paper to 11½" square. Attach the floral paper to the purple pattern paper.

For the cake tiers, cut from the yellow pattern paper, a 4"x11" piece, a 4"x9" piece, and a 4"x8" piece. Edge all three pieces with purple pattern paper.

Trim two ½" strips of pink stripe paper with decorative scissors and drape the top of each yellow layer.

Using a craft knife, trim a flower cluster from the floral paper and use as a cake decoration.

Form the cake by starting at the top and adding the bottom layers. Adhere the cake onto this background.

BIRTHDAY WISHES

Pinwheels Wishes

Materials

1 sheet of Beige Pattern (AG155)
1 sheet of Purple Pattern (AG120)
2 sheets of Purple Floral (AG121)
2 sheets of Purple Stripes (AG143)
3 sheets of Purple Pattern (AG139)
7 lavender brads
Decorative scissors: clouds, sunflower
Screw post

Directions

To create the large pinwheel, cut a 10" square from the purple stripe and the purple pattern papers. Adhere the papers onto each other back-to-back. With decorative scissors, cut along the outside edge of the square. As shown in the Pinwheel Wishes diagram on page 132, cut 3" on the diagonal from the corner toward the center. Punch holes as shown in the diagram. Insert screw post from the back in the center hole. Fold edges with the holes to meet in center. Secure with the top of screw post.

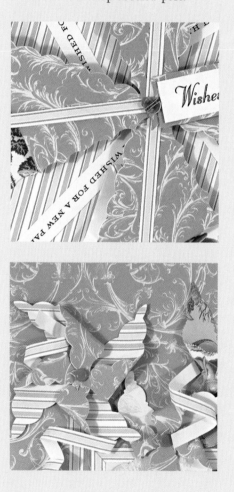

For the smaller pinwheels, use 3" and 4" squares. Instead of a screw post, use brads for the centers. Repeat as before.

For decoration, curl ⅜" purple strips around a pencil. Then add to page with journaling. Frame photo with purple stripes and miter corners.

Secret Wishes

Materials

1 sheet of Blue Pattern (AG126)
1 sheet of Green Pattern (AG074)
1 sheet of Green Solid (AG016)
2 sheets of Blue/Green Pattern (AG134)
6 sheets of Blue/Green Pattern (AG133)
1 die-cut (AG524)
1 die-cut (AG523)
1 frame (AG413)
4 small cream buttons
Decorative scissors: clouds
Thread to match cream buttons

Directions

Cut a 2"x12" strip from blue pattern paper. Using the scoring tool and a ruler, make a score line every ½" along the length of the piece. Pleat by folding on the score lines, forward and backward. Unfold and cut into four ½"x12" strips. Apply double-sided adhesive to the back and pleat again. Attach two pleated pieces end to end with adhesive to form two 12" strips.

Cut a 3½"x12" piece from green pattern paper. Attach the pleated pieces to the top and bottom of this green piece. Then attach to the bottom of the remaining 10"x12" blue pattern piece to form a 12" square.

Cut the blue stripes from all sheets of the blue/green pattern paper. With 5"-long strips, form three Xs in the green section, then trim the excess. Be careful to only apply adhesive on the ends of these strips. Apply two stripes to the top and bottom of the memo board, overlap-ping the pleats. Attach the remaining blue stripes to the background page forming two large intersecting Xs. Remember to apply the adhesive only at the ends of the strips.

Add buttons to the intersections either by sewing with thread or by using foam adhesive.

Using the Secret Wishes template on page 132, create five envelopes from the green pattern paper. Insert journaling into the envelopes, then tuck envelopes and photos into the memo board. Accent with cut-out flowers.

Sweet Sixteen

Materials
1 sheet of Bright Pink Pattern (AG085)
1 sheet of Green Plumes (AG003)
1 sheet of Pink Pattern (AG044)
1 sheet of Pink Pattern (AG054)
1 sheet of Pink Pattern (AG087)

1 sheet of Pink Stripe (AG086)
2 frames (AG411)
Decorative buckle or ornament
Decorative paper clips
Decorative scissors: mini scallop, scallop, sunflower, Victorian
Gold craft wire
Wired-edged pink/green taffeta ribbon

Directions
Trim bright pink pattern paper to an 11½" square with decorative scissors and mount onto light pink pattern paper. Use this as a mat for an 11"-square piece of green pattern paper.

Using the decorative scissors and the Sweet Sixteen template on page 132, make envelopes from four different pink pattern papers. Insert wishes and photos inside envelopes.

Place ribbon and buckle/ornament at the bottom of page. Twist wire to form loops. Attach paper clips to the ends of wire and insert envelope into the clips.

CAPTURE THE MOMENT

Time of Birth

Materials
1 sheet of Green Floral (AG073)
1 sheet of Green Floral (AG076)
2 sheets of Blue Floral (AG065)
3 sheets of Aqua Pattern (AG055)
Border punch
Green satin ribbon
Ivory satin ribbon

Directions

Place a sheet of aqua pattern paper and a sheet of green floral paper with the printed sides together. Cut 1½" strips on a diagonal.

Place all the aqua strips back to form a square. Then weave the green strips into the aqua to form a harlequin pattern. The green strips will go over and then under the aqua strips.

To make the clocks, photocopy the Time of Birth templates on page 132 and cut out. Draw clock hands to indicate the time of birth.

On the back of the sheet of green pattern paper, mark every ⅜" and every ⅝" with a pencil. Using the scoring tool and ruler, score the entire sheet along these marks. Fold along the score lines, alternating forward and then backward to form the pleats.

Unfold the pleated sheet and cut into 1" strips. Apply adhesive to the back of each piece, then pleat again. Attach to the photo mats to form a border. Miter the pleated corners.

Birthday Presents

Materials
1 sheet of Black Floral (AG103)
1 sheet of Gold Pattern (AG027)
1 sheet of Green Pattern (AG073)
1 sheet of Pink Pattern (AG085)
3 frames (AG411, AG413, AG417)
Decorative scissors: mini scallop
Pink taffeta ribbon
Seam-binding ribbons: gold, green

Add photos and title. Using taffeta ribbon, tie a bow for the top of the page.

Newspaper Headlines

Directions

To make the presents, cut the following pieces: 3"x8" and 2"x4" from gold pattern paper, 2"x4" and 1"x2" from green pattern paper, and 2"x3½" from pink pattern paper. Fold each piece in half and journal on the inside.

Wrap a ribbon around the front of the present and add a bow at the top. Using decorative scissors, cut a small tag for each gift.

To make the streamers, curl several ¼" strips of pink pattern paper by wrapping around a pencil.

Materials

1 sheet of Black/Gold Pattern (AG034)
1 sheet of Black Stripe (AG060)
1 sheet of Ivory Pattern (AG071)
3 sheets of Black Floral (AG059)
Black card stock
Ivory satin ribbon

Directions

Photocopy a page from the newspaper on your birthday onto ivory paper and cut to 10¾"x11" to form the background of your page. Mount this sheet onto black floral paper.

Type your journaling to look like a newspaper column, capturing the day's

headlines and the things that you did on your birthday. Frame the text with black stripes and miter the corners.

Using a craft knife, cut out the same flowers from two sheets of the black floral paper. Layer the same flower images on top of each other to create three-dimensional, layered flowers.

Embellish with a "Happy Birthday" tag and a satin bow.

Valentine's Day

TRADITIONS

Love is a canvas furnished by nature
and embroidered by imagination.

Voltaire

One of the first things I remember learning how to make was a paper heart. It's funny that folding and cutting would later become an integral part of my career. In the following scrapbook layouts, I have taken paper heart-making to a whole new level. Enjoy weaving your Valentine's Day memories into your favorite album.

Lonely Hearts Club
DINNER 2003 | NEW YORK CITY

Woven Hearts

A VALENTINE'S TRADITION

Inspired by the fancy hearts
I made as a child from lacy doilies,
I have woven valentines to create
scrapbook pages that are sure
to capture your heart.
Who will be your Valentine this year?

Lonely Hearts Club

DINNER 2003 | NEW YORK CITY

Lonely Hearts Club

I've broken a few hearts in my time
and had my heart broken as well.
But when I am without a sweetheart on
Valentine's Day, you can find me
out with the girls. Commemorate a
Valentine's Day with friends by making
broken hearts with fancy pleats
and interwoven borders.

TRACEY, COLLEEN,
ANGIE, COURTNEY AND
I OUT ON THE TOWN,
FOR VALENTINE'S DAY

Sisterly Love

ANNA AND MISSY IN JUNE 1976

Sisterly Love

Some say that sisters are different
flowers from the same garden.
My mother loved to take our "sister"
pictures all dressed up in her garden.
Fill this woven heart-shaped pocket
with something that you love—
your favorite memories.

My Heart
Belongs to Daddy

MY FIRST DANCE
RECITAL
1971

*My Heart Belongs
to Daddy*

I remember my first dance recital
like it was yesterday. Even though
my mom forgot my tights, I was still
the star of the show. We sang "My
Heart Belongs to Daddy" and danced
our little hearts out. An intricately
woven heart makes the perfect mat
for my photos. Just like my
costume, it's pretty in pink.

WOVEN HEARTS

Lonely Hearts Club

Materials

1 sheet of Red/Gold Pattern (AG025)
2 sheets of Red Pattern (AG002)
2 sheets of Red Stripe (AG095)
3 sheets of Gold Pattern (AG027)
4 sheets of Red/Cream Pattern
   (AG096)
Gold satin ribbon

Directions

To make the borders, cut the intertwining vines from the red/cream pattern paper, using a craft knife. Cut ¼" strip from the red stripe paper. At the intersection of the intertwining vines cut a small slit to weave the red stripe through.

Cut a large heart from the red pattern paper. On the back of the heart, mark every 1" around the outside edge with a pencil. Cut a zigzag down the center for the broken heart.

Apply double-sided adhesive to the back side edges of the heart. Using a 1" red stripe, pleat around the heart by making a fold at every pencil mark. You will need two 12" strips for each side of the heart. To pleat the frames, mark every ½" and

every 1" with a pencil on the back of a sheet of red stripe paper. Be careful to make marks perpendicular to the stripes. Score, with a scoring tool and a ruler, along these marks. Pleat by folding forward and backward along the score lines.

Unfold the pleats and cut 1"-wide strips. Apply adhesive to the back and pleat again. Apply as a border behind the photos. Accent the page with smaller cut-out hearts and a gold bow.

Sisterly Love

Materials
1 sheet of Pink Pattern (AG054)
1 sheet of Pink Pattern (AG082)
2 sheets of Green Pattern (AG073)
3 sheets of Pink/Yellow Floral (AG017)

Directions
To make the woven-heart pocket, fold the pink pattern papers in half. Use the Sisterly Love template on page 133 to cut the two sides of the woven heart from two different pink pattern papers.

On the folded edge, make ½"-wide cuts, 4" into the heart, as shown on the template. Weave the body of the heart to make a pocket. Start by placing the sides one on top of the other to form a heart.

Take the innermost strip from right side of the heart and insert inside the first folded strip on the left side of the heart.

Now, insert the second folded strip (on the left side of the heart) inside the first folded strip from the right side of the heart. Repeat by alternating between these two steps—inside one strip; outside the next strip.

Using a craft knife, cut flowers from the floral paper. Insert the flowers inside the woven-heart pocket along with matted photos and journaling.

My Heart Belongs to Daddy

Materials
1 sheet of Floral (AG012)
1 sheet of Green Pattern (AG039)
1 sheet of Pink Pattern (AG054)
1 sheet of Pink Pattern (AG082)
2 sheets of Pink Pattern (AG085)
Pink satin ribbon

Directions
To make the heart, use a 12"-square piece of ivory card stock as a base, and weave an entire sheet of decorative paper. Begin by choosing three decorative papers (A, B, and C), then cutting ⅜"-wide strips from the following: 28 strips of paper A, 14 strips of paper B, 14 strips of paper C. Lay vertical strips across the width of the card stock in the following order: A, B, A, C, repeating across the entire 12"-square card stock.

For the horizontal strips, weave them in the following manner: Row 1: Using A, go under 1, over 1, under 2, over 2, then continuing by 2s across the page. Row 2: Using B, go under 1, over 1, under 1, over 1, then continuing by 1s across the page. Row 3: Using A, go over 2, under 2, then continuing by 2s across the page. Row 4: Using C, go over 1, under 1, over 3, under 1, over 3, then continuing across the page by 1s and 3s.

Repeat these four rows to weave the entire page. Once the piece is woven, secure by adhering it onto the layer of card stock. Cut a large heart from this sheet, turning the sheet at an angle so the weaving is on the diagonal.

Mount onto a 12"-square piece of floral paper and cut into a heart about 1" larger than the woven heart. Fringe the edge of the floral heart by making small cuts around the entire heart, using scissors. Add your journaling and photos.

Easter

TRADITIONS

The air is like a butterfly with frail blue wings.
The happy earth looks at the sky and sings.

Joyce Kilmer

Easter morning in the Griffin household was all candy and chaos.
Not only did the Easter Bunny leave extravagant baskets filled
with candy and wrapped in colorful cellophane, he left a
clue that sent my sister and I on a hunt around the house.
We went on a wild goose chase for all of our new spring clothes.
The following layouts are inspired by the thrill of the hunt.
I hope you enjoy searching for memories to fill these pages.

The Easter Parade 1971

In your Easter Bonnet with all the frills upon it,

You'll be the grandest lady in the Easter Parade!

The Easter Parade 1971

In your Easter Bonnet
with all the frills upon it,

You'll be the grandest lady
in the Easter Parade!

Easter Parade

Easter morning would not have been
complete without a fancy new outfit
to wear to church. Our family Easter
photo was one of the few times a year
that we would all get dressed up, including
Daddy. What a lucky fellow he was to
have his three lovely ladies by his side!
In this spirit, I have "hidden" photos on
this page. Pull the tabs at the top to
reveal another set of pictures.

Happy Easter
1974

Easter Basket

Each year my small town hosted an
Easter egg hunt. Colorful eggs were hidden
all over the church yard. With my Easter
basket in hand, I loved to run around
searching for eggs. On this scrapbook
page, I re-created my woven Easter basket
from paper and ribbon. The spring grass
made from tissue paper takes me back to
that wonderful time in my life.

Easter Surprises!

Easter Flowers

Easter in the South marks the beginning of Spring and all the flowers are in bloom. My grandmother always cut Easter lilies, crocuses, and jonquils from her yard this time of year. They made her house smell incredible! Just as our Easter presents were hidden, I have hidden the photos on my scrapbook page in grandmother's flowerpots. My memories will bloom for years to come.

Below every Easter Basket was a clue from the Easter Bunny where to find more treasures and gifts. My sister and I would spend all morning hunting for spring clothes.

Easter
TRADITIONS

TREASURE HUNT

Easter Parade

Materials
1 sheet of Blue Stripe (AG066)
1 sheet of Gold Pattern (AG029)
2 sheets of Blue Floral (AG065)
3 sheets of Aqua Pattern (AG055)
4 frames (AG413)
Cardboard
Decorative scissors: Victorian
Green seam-binding ribbon

Directions

Make a grid by marking the following measurements on the back of a sheet of floral paper. Using a pencil, draw vertical lines at 1¼", 5½", 6½", 10¾".

Using a pencil, draw horizontal lines at ½", 2½", 2¾", 4¾", 5", 7", 7¼", 9¼", 9½", 11½". Repeat on the front side of two sheets of aqua pattern paper.

Cut four ⅜"x12" strips from cardboard. Adhere each piece onto the top of the vertical lines on the front of a sheet of aqua pattern paper.

With the remaining sheet of aqua pattern paper with the vertical lines, cut out the two 3¼"x12" vertical strips. Back each strip with a piece of the same pattern paper.

Attach photos and journaling to these two strips inside the horizontal lines. On each strip place, from top to bottom, photo 1, photo 2, caption to go with photo 1, and caption to go with photo 2. Punch a hole and knot ribbons at the top of each strip.

From the floral sheet, cut four 2"x3¼" rectangles from the center. Then cut two openings at the top of the paper, each centered above these two rectangles.

Assemble the page with foam tape. Place a double layer of foam tape on the cardboard tracks and around the sides and bottom of the page.

Attach the floral page with the windows cut out. Insert photo strips inside the track. You may need to trim the bottom of the strip to fit the track appropriately.

Easter Basket

Materials

1 sheet of Aqua Pattern (AG055)
1 sheet of Green Pattern (AG076)
1 sheet of Pink Floral (AG101)
1 sheet of Yellow Pattern (AG102)
1 sheet of Pink Pattern (AG085)
1 sheet of Yellow Pattern (AG100)
Decorative scissors: scallop
Green tissue paper
Pink satin ribbon

Directions

To make the Easter basket, cut three 1"x9" strips from yellow pattern and nine 1"x4" strips from a second yellow pattern. Stack the 9" strips at the top of your work surface going horizontally.

Next, stack the 4" strips to the left on your work surface going vertically. With a 9" piece of ribbon at the top of your work surface going horizontally, attach a 4" strip of yellow paper in the top-left corner of your work surface at a right angle.

Add the rest of the 4" strips across the ribbon horizontally, alternating the strips over and under the ribbon.

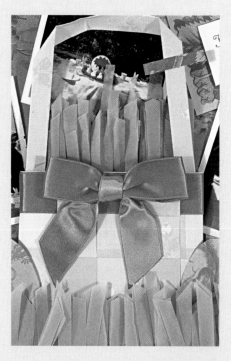

Now, add the 9" strips of yellow paper, alternating the strips over and under the 4" strips. Secure the woven piece by applying adhesive to the edges.

Fold the sides of the woven piece to meet in the back and secure with adhesive. Add a bow to the front of the basket and paper handle.

To make the paper grass, cut and fold an 8"x16" piece of tissue in half to 4"x16". Starting on the side opposite the fold, make 3" cuts every ¼". Trim the edges unevenly. Apply adhesive to the bottom of the page and attach the grass by making small folds every ½". Trim off any excess.

To fill the basket, fold a piece of tissue to 3½"x4". Make cuts as before and insert in the basket.

Use Easter Basket template on page 133 to cut out the eggs from several sheets of decorative paper. Adhere into the basket and the among grass.

Add photos around the eggs and in the basket. Add journaling to a tag and attach it to the basket's handle.

Easter Flowers

Materials

1 sheet of Green Pattern (AG003)
1 sheet of Purple Floral (AG077)
1 sheet of Purple Pattern (AG120)
1 sheet of Purple Pattern (AG139)
1 sheet of Yellow Pattern (AG100)
1 sheet of Yellow Solid (AG122)
1 sheet of Yellow Pattern (AG123)
2 frames (AG412)
2 large silver eyelets & eyelet setter
Plastic template: wavy-edged
Sage green card stock
Yellow sheer ribbon

Directions

Use a plastic wavy-edged template to cut on all four sides of yellow pattern paper to make an 11¼" square. Do not mount onto the background sheet yet.

Cut three flowerpots from purple pattern paper, using the Easter Flowers template on page 133. Position and adhere onto the wavy-edged background sheet.

Cut a slit through each pot and the background sheet with a craft knife.

For photo pull ups, cut three rectangles 3"x4½" from green pattern paper. Place each on sage green card stock and trim, leaving a narrow border.

Cut three ½"x4" strips from card stock. Adhere along the lower 3" edge of each rectangle to form a stop for the pull-up.

Cut three 3" lengths from ribbon. Adhere onto the back top of each rectangle with transparent tape. Insert rectangle through the slit in the flowerpot from the back of the page. Center and adhere page onto the background.

Using the Easter Flowers template, cut three rims from the purple pattern paper. Adhere onto pots only along lower edge of rim to not interfere with the movement of the pull-up.

Cut flowers from purple floral. Place on page and adhere, using foam squares to give dimension to some flowers. Add photos and journaling on tags.

Vacation

TRADITIONS

I have wandered all my life, and I have travelled;
the difference between the two is this;
we wander for distraction, but we travel for fulfillment.

- Hilaire Belloc

When they travel, either alone or together, my friend Holley and her husband always send postcards to each other. Holley says that the postcards help them to relive their vacation memories over and again. Here, I have designed three interactive layouts that showcase vacation memories without damaging precious memorabilia. Your scrapbook could become a collector's item!

Post Cards
SENT FROM FAR AWAY PLACES

Love Letters
THEY TRAVELED THE
WORLD TOGETHER

Travel Folio

My grandparents loved to travel. They
would send me postcards from all over
the world. I remember running to
the mailbox everyday to see if they had
written to me. I made a collage tribute
to them by tucking their postcards and
photographs into a tiered-pocket folio.

Virginia and Ben

MY GRANDPARENTS
AND THEIR POSTCARDS
FROM THE 1900'S

Memorabilia from our Vacation

Tracey & Josh
Blackberry Farm
February 2002

Vellum Pocket

This simple vellum pocket can
be unzipped to reveal all of your
vacation memorabilia. From photos
and postcards to ticket stubs and
brochures, your keepsakes will be
protected. You can even get a glimpse
of them through the pocket.

Travel Journal

Pack your bags! Similar to folding
your clothes, you can fold paper
to make this portable travel journal.
Postcards and photos easily slide in and
out of the pockets. I like to create one
of these for every trip I take. They look
great both in and out of my scrapbook!

TRAVEL JOURNAL

Vacation
TRADITIONS

Travel Folio

Materials

1 sheet of Gold Journal (AG241)
1 sheet of Gold Pattern (AG027)
1 sheet of Stamps Pattern (AG035)
2 sheets of Black/Cream Pattern
  (AG061)
2 sheets of Black/Cream Stripe
  (AG060)
Silver craft wire

Directions

Cut three panels from the black/cream pattern paper as follows: 3"x10½",

5½"x10½" and 9"x10½". Border the panels on all four sides with the black/cream stripe and miter the corners. On the other two panels, apply the border on the sides and top only.

To make the three-dimensional pocket, cut two 3" squares and two 3"x5½" pieces from the same paper. Fold each piece like an accordion and secure at the bottom like a fan.

Adhere the 3" fan onto the sides of the 3" panel and the 5½" fan onto the 5½" panel, with the pattern facing outward.

Layer the pockets in ascending order and adhere them together as in the photo. Mount onto the base. Fill the pockets with photos and memorabilia.

For the journaling banners, roll one end of a 1"x4½" strip of paper and thread craft wire through the center of the roll and back around itself to secure. Cut a dovetail at the end of the journaling banners as shown.

Insert the journaling banners into the folio pockets and add a title to the front of the folio.

Vellum Pocket

Materials
1 sheet of Green Journal (AG242)
1 sheet of Green Stripe (AG004)
1 sheet of Red Floral (AG024)
9" ivory zipper
Decorative scissors: wavy-edged
Green satin ribbon
Permanent double-sided tape
Stamp
Vellum, 11"x17"

Directions
Cut vellum to 10¼"x15¾". Score horizontally along the 15¾" side at 1" and 9" with a burnishing tool. Fold on scores to make a pocket.

Place zipper between ends of the vellum pocket with the zipper underneath the vellum. Trim the ends of the zipper as needed. Adhere zipper with permanent double-sided tape, and adhere both sides of the pocket.

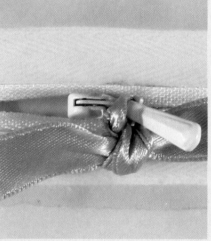

Fill the pocket with your photos and memorabilia. Cover the edges of the pocket with ½" strips of the green stripe paper. Miter the corners.

Create journaling blocks by cutting out a piece of green stripe paper with decorative scissors. Adhere journaling onto top and punch a hole through both layers. Attach block to the zipper pull with a green satin bow.

Create a title in the same manner as the journaling block and attach to the top of the page with foam dots.

Travel Journal

Materials

1 sheet of Brown Solid (AG111)
1 sheet of Gold Journal (AG241)
1 sheet of Sepia Pattern (AG114)
2 sheets of Red Pattern (AG115)
4 sheets of Brown Pattern (AG110)
4 sheets of Wheat Pattern (AG040)
Cardboard
Gold eyelet & eyelet setter

Directions

To make the luggage straps, cut two 1" strips from the red pattern paper. For the buckles, cut two 1¾" squares from the brown solid paper. Cut two parallel 1¼" slits in each square, ⅜" from the top and ⅜" from the bottom. Slide over the red paper "straps."

To make the journal covers, cut two 5"x6½" pieces from cardboard. Cut two 6"x7½" pieces from wheat pattern paper.

Cover each piece of cardboard by centering cardboard on the paper. Fold in each corner of the paper to form right angle and adhere onto cardboard. Then, fold in each side of the paper and adhere onto the cardboard.

To make the journal pockets, cut a piece of wheat pattern paper and a piece of brown pattern paper to 9"x12". Attach the two sheets back-to-back. Fold as in Travel Journal diagram on page 134 to make pocket pages. Apply adhesive on the pocket edges to secure.

Repeat as many times as desired for additional pages. Attach the pages to

each other back-to-back, then attach the pages inside the covers.

Add your photos and postcards inside the pockets.

Print journaling onto gold journal block, trim, and mount onto brown solid paper. Trim the brown paper slightly larger than the journal block.

To create the luggage tag, attach a small loop of brown solid to the journal block with a gold eyelet. Add your title.

Anniversary
TRADITIONS

*Love does not consist of gazing at each other,
but in looking in the same direction.*

Antoine de Saint Exupery

Since weddings are my primary business, it is always fun for me to
scrapbook wedding and anniversary photos. If you scrapbook for no
other reason than to capture your own wedding, it will be time
well spent. No other place in your scrapbook do you have as
many wonderful memories to record and cherish for a lifetime.

Sallie & Charles Griffin
December 20, 1964

Love Letters
from 1960-1971

Love Letters

AN ANNIVERSARY TRADITION

Taking the time to write a letter really means
you care. Whether it is for a special occasion,
or just because you are thinking of someone,
a letter is a gift of yourself. Share that gift
with generations to come by including
your love letters in your scrapbook.

With this ring

Mr. and Mrs. Joshua James Flammer

Our First Anniversary

Our Second Anniversary

Our Vows

We celebrate our anniversary
each year by reading the vows we made
on our wedding day. Our favorites ones are
tucked safely into each pocket.

lly, the marking of the passa
and wife is marke
These rings ar

Our Vows

For my friend Tracey's wedding
anniversary, she and her husband
reread their wedding vows and write love
letters to each other about which mar-
riage vow was most important to them
that year. The pockets on this scrapbook
page highlight a photo
of their celebration and the sleeve
behind contains the love letter.

Our Third Anniversary

Our Fourth Anniversary

Victoria Elizabeth Coleman

AND

John Edward Burke

True love is a modern day phenomenon which dates back thousand of years, still hearts young and old are intrigued by a true love story about real people.

A look back into the history of the citizens of a community will bring many such stories to light, some happy and some sad. One of the happy accounts involving the medical community of Macon county is the story of Dr. John E. Burke and Victoria Coleman. In 1909, Isabelle and John Burke gave birth to John E. Burke and friends. Virginia and Emmett Coleman gave birth to Victoria Elizabeth.

Growing up in a small community of Macon County, John and Victoria grew up being great friends. They attended the same grade schools and church and With their parents also being friends, the two children were always together.

In 1926, John and Victoria graduated from Macon County Academy and spent the summer following Traveling through the depths of Europe. While in Paris, John first realized he had deep feelings for Victoria, feelings of love. But he knew that his feelings could not be revealed as he and Victoria were going to go their separate ways to college after they returned from their travels.

Educated in private schools, John went straight into medical school upon graduation. And Victoria, who was always adventurous, attended The University of Maryland. The two friends would only see each other on holiday, but it Would seem that they had not spent a moment apart. They kept in touch by writing letters, which we Would now call love letters...

While Victoria was away at college her first year, She realized her feelings for John were more Than just friendship, but with them both being away at school, she did not think he would feel the same way.

The next summer, Victoria returned home from Maryland to be with her mother who was stricken with pneumonia. John was there for Victoria and her mother throughout her last days of life.

John now felt it was time to reveal to Victoria his feelings for her. On the eve before Victoria was to catch the train to Baltimore, he proclaimed his love for his lifelong friend.

Love Storybook

Here, I have created a scrapbook within a scrapbook by making a book chronicling the love story of my friend's parents. Turn the pages back in time by recording those vital details of how they met, what they did when they were dating, and a description of their first house.

Victoria Elizabeth Coleman

AND

John E. Burke

Love Letters

This year, my parents will celebrate their thirty-ninth wedding anniversary. They are as happy today as they were in this picture. To preserve that feeling, I have included some of their love letters on this layout, tucked secretly in vellum envelopes behind the photograph.

Sallie & Charles Griffin
December 20, 1964

Love Letters
from 1960-1971

Anniversary
TRADITIONS

Our Vows

Materials
1 sheet of Platinum Floral (AG042)
1 sheet of Platinum Solid (AG010)
1 sheet of Purple Pattern (AG031)
3 sheets of Platinum Pattern (AG006)
5 sheets of Purple Floral (AG046)
Platinum satin ribbon

Directions
To make the left-hand page, cut four 3½" strips from platinum pattern paper. Using a pencil, mark across each strip the following measurements: ⅝", ⅜", ⅝", ⅜", 1½". Score with a burnishing tool and pleat each strip by folding forward and then backward. Apply adhesive on the back side of all pleats to hold the pleating securely in place.

Adhere each pleated strip along the edges of the platinum solid paper to make a frame. Miter the corners.

Repeat technique with purple pattern paper. Begin by cutting four 2½" strips. Measure and score at ⅞", ¼" ⅞", ¼", ¼". Score with burnishing tool, pleat, and secure with adhesive. Attach pleated strips inside the existing frame, leaving

1¼" border. Miter the corners. Add borders around the photo with satin ribbon. Tie the remaining ribbon in a square knot.

To make the right-hand page, divide a sheet of purple floral paper into 6"-square quadrants, using a pencil and a ruler.

Cut two 6" squares from another sheet of purple floral. Using a craft knife, cut a thumb tab at the top center of each piece. From remaining paper, cut four 2"x6" strips. Pleat strips in an accordion fold and adhere one end of each strip together, then attach strips to the back of each cut square on the left, right, and bottom edges with the patterned paper facing outward. Place adhesive along three sides of the square and adhere onto the quadrant sheet. Repeat this step with the platinum pattern paper. Attach photos to the front of each pocket.

Cut eight 2½"x6" strips from the platinum pattern paper. Mark across each strip the following measurement: ⅝", ⅜", ⅝", ⅜", ⅝". Score with a burnishing tool and pleat each strip. Adhere each pleated strip into the center of the platinum pockets, creating a frame for the photos. Miter the corners. Repeat this step with the purple floral paper.

For journaling cards, cut two 5½" squares from the purple floral and two from the platinum floral. Attach journaling. Fill pockets with anniversary memories.

Love Storybook

Measure and score at ⅜" along the left side of each strip. Punch three ⅛" holes through all pages at this seam.

Thread opposite ends of the ribbon from the front through the top and bottom holes. From the back, thread both ends of the ribbon through the center hole. Tie the ribbon into a bow in the front. Fill book with photos and journaling.

Materials

1 sheet of Platinum Journal (AG243)
2 sheets of Ivory Floral (AG071)
2 sheets of Platinum Solid (AG010)
3 sheets of Platinum Pattern (AG006)
Ivory seam-binding ribbon
White photo corners

Directions

Cut four ½" strips from one sheet of platinum pattern paper. Make a border with the strips around half a sheet of platinum solid. Miter the corners. Journal on a 5"x11" piece of vellum and adhere onto the page.

Apply adhesive to the back of a sheet of platinum solid paper and fold in half to form a double-sided 6"x12" sheet.

Adhere two sheets of ivory floral paper together, back-to-back. Cut into two pieces: one at 5⅞" and one at 6⅛". Cut two pieces from vellum, 5⅞"x12" and 6"x12". Collate these five sheets as the pages.

Love Letters

Materials

1 sheet of Platinum Pattern (AG038)
2 sheets of Platinum Floral (AG042)
2 sheets of Platinum Vellum (AG237)
Platinum seam-binding ribbon

Directions

Use the Love Letters template on page 134 to make two envelopes from printed vellum. Use vellum tape to adhere. Attach ribbon to the flap of the envelope. Insert love letters into the envelopes.

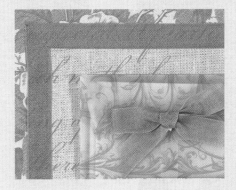

Use ribbon to make a border between the mats and miter the corners.

Using a craft knife, cut out flowers from platinum floral paper and create a frame around the photos.

Thanksgiving
TRADITIONS

Forever on Thanksgiving Day,
the heart will find the pathway home.

~ *Wilbur D. Nesbit*

I love to collect family recipes for those occasions when I have
the time to prepare something special—a meal that transports me
right back to Grandmother's dinner table. Some of my favorite recipes
are those from Thanksgiving—grandmother's cornbread dressing and
pumpkin chiffon pie. Scrapbook pages can be a great way to record your
family's special recipes and celebrate the people who created them.

Mr. Turkey's Wild Ride

ANNA IN CHEROKEE, N.C.
NOVEMBER, 1971

Family Recipes

A THANKSGIVING TRADITION

My Grandmother is the best cook in the whole world! I made these pages to ensure that her recipes can be used for many years to come. I hope you are inspired to scrapbook your family recipes.

Serve in a crystal dish to show off the beautiful color.

Mom's cranberry
not be the most
you've ever
completely d
really sets i
she serves
crystal
every
cranber
with
th
sh

Anna

Cornbread Dressing

Chop 2 onions and cook them in butter in a frying pan. Chop 1 apple and 2 stalks of celery medium fine and add them to the onion. Drain any fat when the apples and celery are soft. Chop day old cornbread into cubes - one loaf should do it. Mix with onions and apples. Add handful of chopped parley, pinch of sage, pinch of thyme, pinch of marjoram and dash

Use 5 good sized sweet
potatoes. Peel them, chop
into cubes and boil them
they're tender when poked
Drain the water off and
them with a fork. Mi:
mashed sweet potatoes
cup of sugar, stick of
a teaspoon of vanilla,
eggs, beaten. Pour i
Pack a cup of brown
and chop a generou:
of pecans. Mix

Sweet Potato Casserole

good sized sweet

Peel them, chop
kes and boil
re tender
the
them

r, a
and 2

Family Recipes

This mini album makes a perfect cook-
book and photo album, all in one.
The recipe tags are protected by a
transparent pocket. Because the recipes
are already tea-stained, you won't be
afraid to use them. This little book
will stand the test of time and can
be passed down for generations.

Family

Recipes

Recipe Wallet

My family photos that I'm most fond of are the ones of us around the dining-room table. My friend Debby's family has this same tradition at Thanksgiving. She and her family are shown here. Combine your photos with your favorite holiday recipes in this vintage paper wallet. It was cleverly weathered using fine sandpaper.

Old Fashioned Bread Stuffing

Ingredients:
* 3-4 loaves of white bread*
* water
* chicken broth
* insides of the turkey
* 2 bunches of celery
* 1 or 2 onions
* 2 TBSP butter
* 1/2 tsp. sage
* oysters (optional)
* mushrooms (optional)

Instructions:
1. The night before you want to eat the stuffing, break the bread into small pieces (about 1 inch squares) into 2 huge bowls or pots. Let the bread sit overnight to dry out.
2. The next day, after you remove the insides of turkey, boil them in water in 2/3 qt. sauce pan until cooked (about 20/30 min

I remember going to Grandma Krull's for thanksgiving Dinner when I was a little girl. The kitchen smelled so good, but was always so hot! Today we still use Grandma's recipes as we gather to give thanks! Dad, Grandma Ogden, Aunt Statia, Grandma Krull, Robin, and I are standing at the table.

November 1965

Mom

Granny

Aunt Evelyn

Corn Bread Dressing

Sage
Pepperidge Farm stuffing mix
Saltine Crackers
Day old cake of Corn Bread
Onion
Cele
Sal
1 k
1/

RECIPES

Recipe Folio

You've organized your closet and
your desk, now organize your recipes
and scrapbook at the same time!
An accordion folder is a great way to
protect your cherished family recipes.
Create index cards with your favorite
photo on one side and a recipe
from your relative on the other.

Thanksgiving Crafts

A THANKSGIVING TRADITION

My Dad was outnumbered in a family of
three women, so football was not very popular
on Thanksgiving at our house. Instead of
watching the game, we would do arts and
crafts. From hand turkeys to headdresses,
we made it all at our kitchen table.
Try incorporating your childhood
crafts into your scrapbook.

GRANDMA DARLENE AND HER TWO TURKEYS!
THANKSGIVING 2002

Hand Turkeys

Turkeys made by tracing my hand always adorned our refrigerator in November. From simple outlines to elaborate layers of construction paper, these were some of my family's most prized possessions. Use this same technique to create grown-up turkeys as embellishments for your scrapbook page.

Mr. Turkey

My parents bought me this Indian headdress on our trip to Cherokee, North
Carolina. I wore it all day and even fell
asleep wearing it. I love this photo of me
on the ferris wheel, I was one happy
little Indian. Create your own feathers
out of different colors of scrapbook
paper. For authentic texture, wrinkle
the paper and then flatten it out.

Mr. Turkey's Wild Ride
ANNA IN CHEROKEE, N.C.
NOVEMBER, 1971

Menu

First Course

Ham B...
Cheese ...
Cham...

Ma...

Fre...

Grandm...

Wh...

Nor...

Missy Griff...

Thanksgiving Headdress

When I look at this picture,
I smile and think about how cute
my sister was as a child. By combining
Thanksgiving memorabilia with
decorative paper, scissors, and raffia,
I have created a scrapbook page that
is just as cute as Missy is!

One little, two little, three little Indians | Missy on Tha...ing, 1975

I'm Thankful For...

A THANKSGIVING TRADITION

On Thanksgiving Day, everyone in my family gathers at the table before the big feast to tell what we are most thankful for. It is a very special event that brings us closer together for the holiday. I have made these pages to share with you some of the things for which I give thanks.

I am
thankful for
friends and
family!

Autumn Thanks

While growing up, my sister and
I had a huge yard to play in.
Our favorite place to play was in
a big pile of leaves that were
collected at the bottom of the driveway.
I cut out a pile of leaves from my
decorative paper as a tribute
to our favorite pastime.

Especially
for Sisters!

Gratitude Folio

My little nephew Charles is so cute,
I just want to put him in my pocket!
I like to create pockets on my
scrapbook pages to hold not just
the pictures, but all of my keepsakes.
With a few simple folds, you can
create this paper pocket to hold
your photos and treasures.

This year I am
thankful for...

My Nephew!

A pocketful
of treasure!

Little Charles
at one year old.
2003

I AM *Thankful* FOR MY *Sister*

Thank-you Card

Being thankful for the relationships
in your life doesn't happen just once
a year. You can make it a weekly
occurrence in your scrapbook.
This beautiful bouquet opens to
reveal a special photo of my sister
and I on vacation last spring.

81

Thanksgiving TRADITIONS

RECIPE BOOKS
Family Recipes

Materials
1 sheet of Brown Solid (AG111)
1 sheet of Gold Floral (AG 049)
1 sheet of Red Pattern (AG115)
1 sheet of Sepia Stripe (AG098)
1 sheet of Sepia Pattern (AG114)
2 sheets of Green Pattern (AG118)
2 sheets of Green Pattern (AG138)
Brown/ivory card stock
Copper eyelet & eyelet setter
Decorative scissors: zigzag
Red gingham ribbon
Spray bottle
Seam-binding ribbons: gold, ivory, red
Snap
Tags
Tea bags
Transparency film

Tip: Be certain to get the transparency film that works best for the type of printer used. The words can also be photocopied onto film at a copy center.

Directions
Tip: This book has seven spreads, but it can be made longer. Simply remember to expand the spine size to accommodate the completed pages.

For each two-page spread, print the name of a person and the name of the recipe onto a transparency. Cut out each, so that the name is on a 3"x4⅝" piece and recipe is on a 4⅝"x5½" piece.

Cut two different green pattern papers for a total of seven pages measuring 6"x9¼". Score and fold in half along the length.

Cut seven 1"x6" strips and seven 4⅝"x3" strips from gold floral paper. Attach 1"x6" floral strips to the sides of each page. Alternate by putting this strip on the right or left side of each page. Attach the 4⅝"x3" pieces to the remaining pages at the bottom. Cut seven ¼" strips from sepia stripe paper.

Position transparencies on the pages and punch ⅛" eyelet holes in the corners through both layers of transparency and paper at the same time. Insert eyelets.

Stack the pages together and measure their width at its highest point. This measurement gives you the height for the spine of the book. Cut one 6¼" piece from card stock by this measurement. Cut two more 4⅝"x6¼" pieces to use as covers. Cut a piece from sepia pattern paper to fit the covers and the spine. Be certain to leave a small space between the cover and the spine to accommodate the pages. Adhere the covers and the spine onto the back side of this paper.

Adhere inner pages together along the outside edges, but not at the top or bottom, of the page. Attach pages to covers in the same manner.

To tea-stain tags and small piece of ivory card stock, brew a strong batch of tea: one pitcher-sized bag to one cup of water. When cool, pour into spray bottle and heavily mist tags and card stock on both sides. Allow to dry. Iron if necessary to flatten them.

Print recipes on tags and the book title on card stock. Mount photos onto tags. Tie ribbons through top of tags. Insert photos and recipe tags into the page pockets. Decorate book cover with red gingham ribbon and snap.

Recipe Wallet

Materials
1 sheet of Black/Gold Pattern (AG034)
1 sheet of Gold Solid (AG029)
1 sheet of Red Pattern (AG050)
1 sheet of Sepia Stripes (AG098)
1 sheet of Sepia Pattern (AG114)
2 sheets of Grey Block Alphabet Stickers
    (AG605, AG606)
2 sheets of Red Floral (AG115)
3 sheets of Brown Pattern (AG110)
Brown elastic
Cardboard
Cream thread
Fine-grit sandpaper
Large cream button

Directions
Cut brown pattern paper to 5½"x12". Adhere onto center of background sheet. Cut two strips from sepia pattern paper. Center and adhere onto each side of brown strip.

To make ribbon border, cut five strips from sepia stripe paper. Mark 1½", then

¾", alternating across each strip. Fold to form paper bows. Cut narrow strips from sepia stripe paper. Cut into 1" sections and adhere onto center of each bow. Piece ribbons together to form border just under each outer edge of strips. Sand edges of papers lightly for an aged look.

Use Recipe Wallet template on page 135 to make the book Cut red pattern paper to 8½"x11" for cover. Score and fold ⅝" in from each side. Open folds. Cut each corner diagonally so sides fold in easily. Cut two 4¾"x7¼" pieces from cardboard. Adhere inside each side of the cover, making certain there is no cardboard down the center of the book.

Cut a strip from the red stripe paper. Center and adhere from inside front cover, around book to inside back cover. Sew button to the cover. Secure loop of elastic to back of book. Sand all edges of book lightly for an aged look.

For pages, cut brown pattern paper to 6¾"x9¼" to make as many pages as you want in the book. Adhere pages together, back-to-front, and onto inside front cover and inside back cover.

To make recipe cards, cut card stock to 3"x5". Attach photos and recipes.

Recipe Folio

Materials
1 sheet of Cream Pattern (AG070)
2 sheets of Red & Brown Floral (AG112)
2 sheets of Red Pattern (AG115)
4 sheets of Gold Pattern (AG027)
3 frames (AG414)
Gold seam-binding ribbon

Directions
Use Recipe Folio template on page 135 to create recipe cards. To reverse the tab, trace pattern onto the reverse side of the paper.

To make recipe folio, cut 6½"x9" piece from cardboard. Score in the center at 4½" to form the folder. Adhere a 24" piece of ribbon in the center, wrapping around the folded edge. Cover with a piece of red/brown floral paper.

To make the accordion sides, cut two 2"x4½" pieces from floral paper. Fold the 2" side every ½" and insert at the sides of the folder, with the pattern facing out. Insert recipe cards and tie closed.

THANKSGIVING CRAFTS

Hand Turkeys

Materials

1 sheet of Dark Green Pattern (AG051)
1 sheet of Gold Pattern (AG027)
1 sheet of Green Pattern (AG138)
1 sheet of Sepia Pattern (AG097)
1 sheet of Sepia Stripes (AG098)
1 sheet of Wheat Pattern (AG040)
2 sheets of Acorns (AG047)

2 sheets of Green Pattern (AG118)
2 sheets of Leaves (AG048)
1 frame (AG417)

Directions

Trace hands onto different patterned papers and cut out. Using a craft knife, cut out leaves from acorn and leaves papers and use them to form the feathers on your hand turkey. Use small leaves to make the beak, wattle, and eyes.

Cut background sheets to 10"x11" and attach 1" strips to the outside edges of the layout. Using scissors, make small cuts in the strips to form fringed edge. Cover overlap with smaller strips and miter the corners.

Mr. Turkey

Materials

1 sheet of Brown Pattern (AG110)
1 sheet of Brown Solid (AG111)
1 sheet of Gold Pattern (AG107)
1 sheet of Red Pattern (AG002)
1 sheet of Red Pattern (AG050)
1 sheet of Sepia Pattern (AG114)
2 sheets of Green Floral (AG116)
2 sheets of Red Floral (AG115)
Brown satin ribbon
Decorative scissors: deckle-edged
Fine-grit sandpaper

Directions

Cut four ½" strips from gold pattern paper. Adhere onto green floral paper, ⅛" from each edge. Cut four ½" strips from brown solid paper, using decorative scissors on one edge of each strip. Adhere onto background sheet, ½" from each edge, over gold pattern strips. Cut four strips from both sheets of red pattern paper. Add to background over deckle-edged strips.

Cut flowers from second sheet of green floral paper. Adhere onto background with foam squares.

Trace your thumb onto gold pattern paper and cut out for the turkey's head.

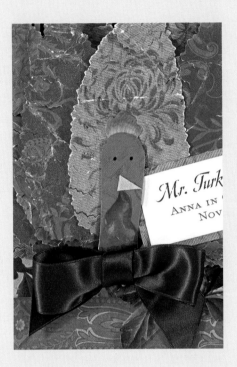

Using decorative scissors, cut feathers from different patterned papers, using the Mr. Turkey template on page 136. Crumple and unfold. Sand lightly. Fold feathers in half and unfold. Cut toward center of each feather with decorative scissors to fringe, being careful to not cut too close to the center fold.

Cut petals from the red and gold flowers on green floral paper to make the turkey's beak, wattle, and eyes. Finish with a satin bow tie and title.

Thanksgiving Headdress

Materials
1 sheet of Brown Pattern (AG110)
1 sheet of Dark Green Pattern (AG051)
1 sheet of Gold Pattern (AG107)
1 sheet of Green Pattern (AG073)
2 sheets of Floral (AG049)
2 sheets of Red Pattern (AG002)
Decorative scissors: sunflower
Raffia

Directions
To make the headdress, cut two 2"x4" pieces from floral paper and adhere them end-to-end. Loop to form an 8" circle, trim any excess, and adhere loop ends together. Tie the raffia around the band.

Using Thanksgiving Headdress template on page 136 and the decorative scissors, cut out nine feathers from different patterned papers.

Attach five feathers to the back of the headdress band and four feathers inside the front of the headdress band. Flatten the circle to attach the headdress to the background page.

Add photos, memorabilia, and journaling to the headdress. Add a title to the front of the headdress band.

I'M THANKFUL FOR...

Autumn Thanks

squares. One square will be used to make the flaps on each side of the mats.

Cut diagonally to make each square into two triangles. Measure from the base of the triangle and mark with a pencil at 3", 3¼", 3¾", and 4". Score lines across the back of the squares along these lines. Fold on the score lines, making a box pleat (fold forward, backward, backward, then forward.) Add adhesive to the back to hold the pleats securely.

The pleats make the sides uneven, so measuring from the corner point, use a ruler or triangle and a craft knife to trim the pleated paper and leave straight sides. Repeat for each flap.

To make the folded mats, cut two 6" squares from brown card stock for bases. Draw an X lightly across the brown card stock, using a pencil, from corner to corner. These lines will help you place your flaps and will be erased later. Hold the flaps in position on the brown card-stock mat. The corner of each piece

should meet in the middle along the X drawn earlier. Score the flap where it will wrap around the edge of the mat. Trim excess, leaving a flap on the back. Attach the flap to the mat block and repeat with remaining flaps.

Cut two 3¼" squares from green pattern paper and from green vine paper. Cut them in half diagonally. Adhere these pieces inside the flaps.

To make the wreath, cut out leaves and acorns, using a craft knife. Layer with foam dots around the photo.

Gratitude Folio

Materials
1 sheet of Green Lettering (AG039)
1 sheet of Leaves (AG048)
1 sheet of Sepia Stripes (AG098)
2 sheets of Green Pattern (AG118)
4 sheets of Acorns (AG047)
Brown card stock

Directions
Cut a sheet of acorn paper into four 6"

Materials
1 sheet of Brown Pattern (AG110)
1 sheet of Green Journal (AG242)
1 sheet of Green Pattern (AG039)
1 sheet of Green Pattern (AG073)
1 sheet of Red Floral (AG024)
1 sheet of Red Pattern (AG050)
1 sheet of Red Stripe (AG095)
Decorative scissors: wide scallop

Directions

To make the memento wallet, cut a sheet of red floral paper to 11¾"x12". Mark, score, and fold on the back of the sheet of paper as follows: across the 11¾" side at 4" and 8" from left side. Then mark 3" and 8½" from the top of the 12" side of the paper.

On the back of the paper, apply double-sided adhesive along outer-right and -left edges of top and bottom thirds of wallet. Fold top down, then fold bottom up, matching side edges. Fold left side in and press folds in place, then fold right side in and press folds in place.

Cut the top and bottom of a sheet of green pattern paper with the decorative scissors and mount the wallet onto it.

On the bottom edge of the scalloped paper, evenly space three punched holes about ¼" up from the tips of the scallops.

Using the thin strips of red stripe paper, string the journal block through the holes punched earlier. Tie the thin paper strips into knots and remove any excess paper strip.

Tuck photos and memorabilia into the memento wallet.

Thank-you Card

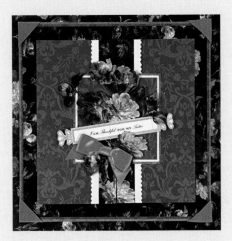

Materials

1 sheet of Gold Floral (AG107)
1 sheet of Gold Journal (AG241)
1 sheet of Gold Pattern (AG027)
3 sheets of Red Pattern (AG002)
4 sheets of Black Floral (AG103)
Decorative scissors: scallop
Gold satin ribbon
Gold satin ribbon corners

Directions

Cut two 7" x 9" pieces from red pattern paper. Trim one of the 9" sides with decorative scissors. Starting at the scalloped side, score and fold backward at 1½"and forward at 6" to form a Z. Repeat for the other piece.

Cut a 10"x11" piece from black floral paper. Make a fold 1" in from the edge on both 11" sides.

Attach the red folded piece underneath the folded side of the black floral to form a gate-folded card. The folds with decorative edges should meet in the center.

Use red pattern paper to cover the inside edges. Use black floral paper to accent the front where the folded sides meet in the center.

Cut flowers from the black floral paper. Mount and attach to the left side of the gate-fold with journaling and a bow.

Add photos and journaling inside the gate-folded card.

Christmas
TRADITIONS

*What is Christmas? It is tenderness for the past,
courage for the present, hope for the future.
It is a fervent wish that every cup may overflow
with blessings rich and eternal, and
that every path may lead to peace.*

- Agnes M. Pharo

On Christmas, I can still feel the excitement I felt as a child
when I awoke to find beautifully wrapped presents under the tree.
Since then, I have learned that Christmas is not just a holiday for
children, it is for all of us who are young at heart. Capture the spirit
of the season with some of my favorite holiday traditions.

Happiest of Holidays
Little Anna · 1968

Holiday Cards

A CHRISTMAS TRADITION

Photo cards adorn the mantel, the
refrigerator, and even the card basket
in our house at Christmastime. It's great
to see pictures of people and families
and how they've changed year after year.
This year, instead of tossing them out,
use them to decorate your scrapbook!

HOLIDAY GREETINGS

KISSES AT CHRISTMAS!

Cards are one of my favorite things about the holidays. We all give each other a card on Christmas Eve.

Paper Wreath

My mother loves to tell the story about when this photo was taken. I wouldn't stop trying to sing Christmas carols—"fa la la la la, la la la la—as all I could manage! I've used cut-out flowers from decorative paper to make a three-dimensional wreath to frame my treasured holiday photo.

91

Christmas Kisses

Christmas Kisses

This picture captures the essence of the holidays and the excitement most of us felt as a child. Pictured here is my little friend Jack, decking the halls with boughs of holly. Create your own garland border by adhering two sheets of paper back-to-back. Cut into the shape of a holly leaf and fold in half for a little dimension.

Under the Mistletoe

Daddy sneaking a kiss under the mistletoe with Mom always made my sister and I giggle. If we had only taken their picture. This is a tradition I recommend that you start early! Here's little Jack again, this time stealing his first kiss!

Jack's First Kiss · Christmas 2002

On the tag: *Christmas Festivities 2002*

On the card (window 8): *Baby Charles has the Christmas spirit! December 08, 2002*

Window numbers: 1, 2, 3, 7, 8, 9, 10, 17, 18, 19, 20

Advent Calendars

A CHRISTMAS TRADITION

Every night in December, my sister and I would take turns opening a door on our advent calendar, counting down the days until Christmas. For a great holiday scrapbook twist, record what you do each day to celebrate the season behind each window. You'll have a holiday treasure to look back on for years.

All Through
the House . . .

This paper house is full of
Christmas memories. My photos
and journaling are located behind
each window. By opening them,
I let the holiday spirit out no
matter what time of year it is.

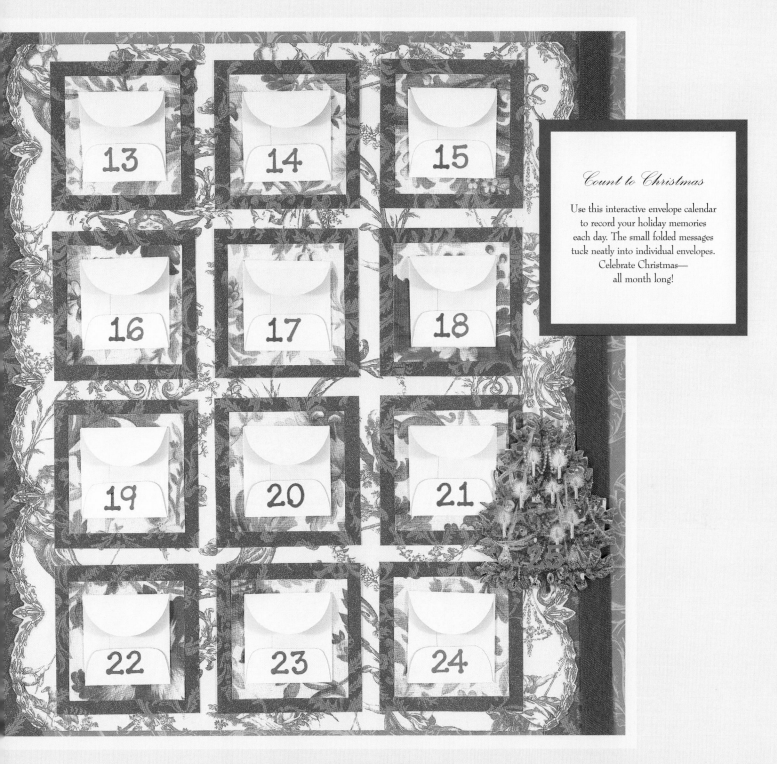

Count to Christmas

Use this interactive envelope calendar
to record your holiday memories
each day. The small folded messages
tuck neatly into individual envelopes.
Celebrate Christmas—
all month long!

Visions of Sugarplums Danced in Their Heads...

OUR CHRISTMAS COOKIES 2002

Cookies!

A CHRISTMAS TRADITION

My sister and I loved to help our
mother make cookies for the holidays.
From gingerbread men to sugar angels, we
would decorate the cookies
just like we had decorated the tree.
Use the shape of your cookie
cutters as paper page accents.

CHRISTMAS SUGAR COOKIES
2 c UNSIFTED ALL-PURPOSE FLOUR
1/4 c SUGAR
1/4 TS SALT
1/2 c BUTTER
1 LARGE EGG
1 TSP VANILL

1. PREHEAT O
2 BAKING SH
2. IN LARGE

CHRISTMA
1 BASIC CH
1/3 c MOLAS
1/2 TSP BAK
1/2 TSP GRO
TSP GRO

2. DIVID
KE TH
FACE RO
3" COOKI
BAKING S

4. BAKE
BROWN.
DECORA

MAKES 3 DOZEN

6. BAKE
7. TRANS
DESIREE
COLORE

MAKES 1

Visions of Sugarplums

My grandmother always wore a blue
apron when she was in the kitchen.
She made everything from scratch,
even cookies! This layout was inspired
by that beautiful linen apron that
she wore; and I can still smell those
cookies baking. Use decorative scissors
to dress up your page and make a vellum
apron to hold all your cookie recipes.

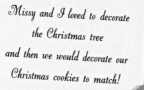

Missy and I loved to decorate the Christmas tree and then we would decorate our Christmas cookies to match!

CHRISTMAS 1979

Christmas Trees

Decorating the Christmas tree was the highlight of the holiday for me. My mom collected two ornaments every year, since the year I was born. One for me, and the other for Missy. She recently gave me my collection so that I could start my own decorating traditions. A tree-shaped cookie cutter makes three trees for my scrapbook, all decorated with paper sprinkles!

**Christmas
1968**

Gingerbread Men

The smell of gingerbread always
reminds me of Christmas. My sister
and I loved making a gingerbread
house every year and decorating it
with candy canes and gumdrops.
For this layout, a traditional
gingerbread man cookie-cutter shape
is adorned with paper icing made
from quilled pieces of paper.

Anna & Missy, sisters
under the Christmas tree.
Our favorite cookies were
gingerbread men, mother
would make them for us
every year at Christmas.

Christmas
TRADITIONS

HOLIDAY CARDS

Paper Wreath

Materials

1 sheet of Gold Journal (AG241)
2 sheets of Gold Pattern (AG027)
2 sheets of Red Pattern (AG050)
4 sheets of Red Floral (AG024)
3 die-cuts (AG517)
Gold cord
Red wired-edged taffeta ribbon

Directions

To make the wreath, use a craft knife to cut ten clusters of flowers from three sheets of red floral paper.

Attach photo to the page, then layer all of the flowers on top to form a circle. Use foam tape for a three-dimensional effect. Tie a bow at the top of the wreath. Attach journaling tag with a gold cord.

On the second page, attach a 4" piece of gold pattern paper to the right side of an 11" square of red pattern paper. Use ribbon to cover the seam where the red and gold paper meet in the background, then mount to a sheet of red floral paper.

Cut out more red flowers for the border. Layer flowers for a three-dimensional effect. One or more pieces of foam tape can be applied, depending on the height desired.

Cover the ribbon with die-cut flowers and insert photos and cards.

Christmas Kisses

Cut berries from holly paper and adhere between leaves with foam squares.

To make the card, attach photo to folded colored card stock and mount in the center of the page.

Use the small holly punch to make the small holly leaves. Layer with red berries on the title banner. Use Christmas Kisses template for banner shape. Use stickers to create the title.

Under the Mistletoe

Materials

1 sheet of Dark Green Pattern (AG051)
1 sheet of Green Pattern (AG118)
1 sheet of Holly Pattern (AG105)
1 sheet of Red Pattern (AG050)
1 sheet of Red Stripe (AG095)
1 sheet of Poinsettia Pattern (AG106)
2 sheets of Green Script Alphabet
   Stickers (AG609, AG610)
Holly punch

Directions

Using Christmas Kisses template on page 136, cut sixteen holly leaves from dark green paper. Adhere eight of the leaves along three sides of the page as shown above.

Fold the remaining eight leaves in half lengthwise, right sides together. Fold open, rolling the leaves back from the center crease. Add foam squares and attach to the top of the first set of leaves, using the foam squares to keep the creases in place.

Materials

1 sheet of Green Pattern (AG051)
2 sheets of Red Pattern (AG050)
3 sheets of Holly (AG105)
8 red satin ribbon corners
Circle cutter
Green ink pad
Rubber stamp: Christmas greetings

Directions

Cut a 6"x12" piece from red pattern paper. Score the paper so it folds in half, making a card that is 6" square. Using a circle cutter, cut a 3" circle in the front of the card.

Cut a 5¾"-square piece of ivory card stock. Cut a 2¾" circle in the center of it. Mount ivory circle inside the front cover of the card. Attach photo behind the ivory circle. Stamp a Christmas sentiment inside the card.

Using a craft knife, cut out holly from the sheet of patterned paper.

Arrange them into a wreath shape around the card opening, allowing the edges of the holly to overlap the opening for a more realistic look. Use foam adhesive to add dimension.

Mount the card to the page, using satin ribbon corners. Use holly cut from the patterned paper to make a border around the page.

ADVENT CALENDARS

All Through the House

Materials
2 sheets of Brown Pattern (AG110)
2 sheets of Brown Solid (AG111)
2 sheets of Dark Green Pattern (AG051)
3 sheets of Red Pattern (AG050)
Card stock: black, navy, yellow
Christmas Tree Die-cut (LC409)
Decorative scissors: stamp
Ivory seam-binding ribbon
Mini brass brads

Punches: medium cat, small holly, sunflower
Yellow decorative chalk

Directions
Cut two pieces from brown pattern paper for the body of house, using the Advent Calendars template on page 137. Cut out window and door openings. Cut two pieces from brown solid paper for the roof of the house, following the template.

Cut 18 rectangular window frames, using the Advent Calendars templates on page 138 from dark green pattern paper. Also cut seven dormer (pointed) window frames, following the templates.

To make the hinges, trace the outline of the window frame, then add a ½"-wide tab to one side of the window. This tab mounts to the window opening cut into the body of the house so that the window can open and reveal the journaling or photos. Score between the frame shape and the tab to make the opening easier.

Cut strips from red pattern paper with decorative scissors to make curtains for the eighteen rectangular windows.

Layer the curtains beneath the window frames. If that window has the tree die-cut or the cat punch, add that below the frame. Apply the frame and curtain assembly onto the hinged base.

Add windows to the body of the house by tucking the window tab under the edge of the window opening.

For the dormer windows, cut six pieces from ivory card stock the same size as the frames. Because the roof under these windows is brown, this piece becomes the surface for journaling. The center

window will be cut in half after assembly to be divided onto the two pages as shown below left. It does not lift up and does not need an ivory base.

Apply black tabbed window base to the ivory piece, folding the tab under the ivory base. On front of black base, add pieces of red pattern paper as candles. Chalk the black card stock above it to create the halo for the candlelight. Add yellow card stock pieces from sunflower punch as flames. Add green window frame over assembly.

For chimneys, cut two pieces from the red pattern paper, following the template. Cut strips from brown pattern paper, following the template and add to the top.

Apply adhesive to the chimneys only around the edges, so that they make a pocket. Cut narrow ivory tag and add seam-binding ribbon to the top. Insert the tag into the chimney.

Cut doors, following the template, then make door liners from ivory card stock. Just like when making the window lin-

ers, be sure to add a hinge. The tab should be on different sides for each door so that the doors each open from the center.

Insert brass brads as doorknobs before attaching the liners to the doors to camouflage the backs of the brads.

Cut small rectangles to create the raised-panel look. Apply them to the door with foam adhesive. Print "25" onto a small square and add to the top of one door.

Punch holly leaves from green pattern paper and add to the door in wreath shape, applying wreath around the door number. Add doors to the house. Cut the steps and door frame from brown solid and use foam adhesive to attach.

For the windowsills, print the numbers of the days of the month onto brown solid paper. Cut these pieces to size as shown on template. Add them to the windows, being careful to put them on in the correct order.

Add journaling and photos inside the windows, doors, and chimney tags.

Count to Christmas

Materials
1 sheet of Gold Pattern (AG027)
1 sheet of Red Floral (AG024)
1 sheet of Green Border Stickers
    (AG614)
1 sheet of Red/Gold Pattern (AG025)
2 sheets of Green Pattern (AG118)
2 sheets of Green Floral (AG119)
2 sheets of Red Pattern (AG050)
2 sheets of Green Script Alphabet
    Stickers (AG609, AG610)

Christmas Tree Die-cut (LC409)
Gold number stickers
Red seam-binding ribbon

Directions
Place a border sticker along the left side of the green floral paper. Trim along the scallops, then cut to 9¼"x11½".

With second sheet of green floral paper, place a sticker on one side and trim along scallop. Place sticker on opposite side 9½" away from existing side. Trim along scallop and cut height to 11½".

Cut three 2"x12" strips from red pattern paper. Place one on green pattern sheet 1½" from left edge. Center 14" of ribbon over the left edge of the strip, adhering ends onto the back of the page. Attach scallop sheet to page.

With remaining red strips, adhere onto a second page of green pattern paper ¾" from the right and left edges. Attach ribbon and scallop sheet.

Using the Count to Christmas template on page 138, make 12 envelopes from red/gold pattern paper and 12 envelopes from gold pattern paper. Cut them out, score, fold, and adhere them.

Make note cards for each envelope from a 2¾"x1⅜" piece of folded gold pattern paper. Insert a note card into each envelope with your journaling on it.

Adhere the envelopes onto the page and number them for each day of the month. Embellish the page with a die-cut Christmas tree.

COOKIES!

Visions of Sugarplums

Materials
1 sheet of Blue Pattern (AG117)
1 sheet of Cream Pattern (AG041)
1 sheet of Green Floral (AG116)
2 sheets of Blue Pattern (AG126)
2 sheets of Blue Stripe (AG141)
4 sheets of Blue Floral Stripe (AG127)
2 medium cream buttons
Blue seam-binding ribbon

Cookie cutters: angel, Christmas tree, gingerbread man, rocking horse
Decorative scissors: wide scallop
Punches: lattice border, snowflake
Silver paper
Vellum

Directions
Cut eight strips from two sheets of blue floral stripe paper. Adhere each strip to blue pattern paper and trim along each edge, using decorative scissors.

Cut vellum to 8½"x7½". Make a forward fold 2" from the top. Use punch to create a border. Attach vellum to page, then attach blue scalloped border. Insert recipes and photos.

Trace cookie cutters onto silver paper. Cut out. Place silver cutouts on blue pattern paper and trim, leaving an even border around edges.

Adhere silver cutouts onto shapes with foam squares. Cut blue flowers from green floral paper and use to decorate cutouts. Punch snowflakes from blue floral paper and use to decorate cutouts.

Add blue bows to cutouts before adhering them onto the page.

Christmas Trees

Materials
1 sheet of Red Pattern (AG162)
2 sheets of Green Pattern (AG163)
2 sheets of Ivory Pattern (AG155)
2 sheets of Gold Pattern (AG027)
Cookie cutters: Christmas trees
Decorative scissors: scallop
Mini punches: variety
Scrap paper

Directions
Use cookie cutters to trace, then cut two tree shapes from green pattern paper and one from gold pattern paper. Cut frosting for the tree cookies from pattern papers, two gold and one ivory, making them slightly smaller than the trees. Use the mini punches to create the decorative sprinkles from scrap paper. Adhere them onto the frosting layers of the cookies.

Adhere the cutouts onto the page. Mat photos with a decorative edge and adhere onto the page around the tree cutouts.

For the garland, cut eighteen ¼"x2" strips from the green and gold pattern papers. Create a loop by applying adhesive to one end and adhering ends. Insert the next strip through the first loop before adhering it. Repeat to form the garland chain.

Drape the garland across the top of the page and adhere in place. Add journaling among the photos and tree cutouts.

Missy and I loved to decorate the Christmas tree and then we would decorate our Christmas cookies to match!

CHRISTMAS 1979

Gingerbread Men

Materials
1 sheet of Cream Pattern (AG155)
1 sheet of Dark Green Pattern (AG051)
1 sheet of Gold Pattern (AG107)
1 sheet of Ivory Pattern (AG155)
2 sheets of Red Pattern (AG050)
⅛" quilling papers: white, red
Brown card stock
Cookie cutter: gingerbread man
Gold cord
Needle quilling tool

Directions
Trace cookie cutters and cut out gingerbread men from brown card stock.

To make scrolling icing lines, use a needle quilling tool. Lay white paper across the top of the tool at a 45-degree angle to the tool, with the end of the paper pointing away from the handle toward the top of the tool. Use left thumb to hold paper against the needle, while turning the handle of the tool with the right hand, so that the paper continues to wrap around the tool as it turns. (Reverse hand positions for the left-handed.)

The paper will slide its way off the top of the tool in the scroll shape as the tool is turned. Slow, even turning produces the best results.

When finished, apply the scrolling line to the edges of the cookie cutouts, using a thin line of glue on the edges of the cutout to adhere it. If more than one piece is needed, piece them together on the cutout, trying to match the direction of the scrolling.

To make the eyes, use tight coil shapes. Wrap the paper around the quilling tool and turn the tool handle. Keep the paper directly over the paper below it to build up a disk of coiled paper. Each eye is made of 5" from white quilling paper.

Add glue to the end of the paper and press down to the coil before removing it from the tool. Attach to the cutout.

To make the buttons, attach 3" of red paper to 3" of white paper, then coil.

To make the journal tags cut tag shapes from brown card stock and apply journaling on ivory paper to the tags. Punch a hole in one end of the tag and string gold cord through the hole. Tie the ends in a knot.

Christmas 1968

Anna & Missy, sisters under the Christmas tree. Our favorite cookies were gingerbread men, mother would make them for us every year at Christmas.

To make the candy-cane border, cut ⅜"x12" strips from red and ivory pattern papers. Attach a strip of red and a strip of ivory together side by side with a piece of tape on the back. Add another piece of tape to the back so that it hangs off the edge at least ¼".

Wrap the strip around a pencil on a diagonal, sliding the pencil out as you go. As you twist, the strips will adhere onto the exposed tape. Trim the four candy canes to the same exact size and form a square in the center of the page. Place the tags and the gingerbread men over the corners.

New Year's

TRADITIONS

Each age has deemed the new-born year
The fittest time for festal cheer.

- Sir Walter Scott

I believe that the start of a fresh New Year is a great time to evaluate
where I am and what I have accomplished in the year gone by.
In addition to celebrating, I like to create fortunes for my party
guests and even save the champagne cork wire to use as an
embellishment on my scrapbook page. Adopt one of the
traditions illustrated on the pages that follow to make
the beginning of your year extraordinary!

Champagne Wishes

A NEW YEAR'S TRADITION

Make a toast to the ones you love the most.
"To the New Year and new ideas!"
You too can celebrate the New Year
with these elegant scrapbook page ideas
by turning our traditions into yours.

Hallie, Allen and Evelyn
New Year's Eve 1979
My Grandparents
Fiftieth Wedding Anniversary

FAITH

HOPE

A Toast

My grandparents always celebrate special occasions with champagne. To commemorate my grandparents' fiftieth wedding anniversary, I have decorated the page with a few contemporary embellishments. Silver wire and tags add a certain festivity to the traditional gold color scheme used for a fiftieth anniversary.

Treasured Moments

I cannot think of a better way to ring
in the New Year than an evening with
close friends. I saved the wire from our
champagne cork—it's just the thing
to make a page pop! To make the page
even more festive, I have made a pop-up
card in the center of the layout.

Treasured Memories

Happy New Year!

Timeless Moments

Good Fortune

A NEW YEAR'S TRADITION

My friend Tracey's family always celebrated on New Year's Day by eating Chinese food. Her favorite part of the meal was the fortune cookie. In the coming pages, the scrapbook layouts show you how to bring your family a bit of good fortune in the coming year.

IF YOU DON'T FAIL NOW AND AGAIN, IT'S A SIGN YOU'RE PLAYING IT SAFE.

EN IT GETS DARK ENOUGH, YOU CAN SEE THE LIGHT.

BE GENTLE TO ALL AND STERN WITH YOURSELF.

Y IS THAT IN WHICH YOU HAVE NOT LAUGHED.

FAMILY FORTUNES

Family Fortunes

My sister and her husband
write fortunes for each other and
exchange them on New Year's Eve.
I made this giant cookie to hold
their fortunes by tracing a dinner
plate onto decorative paper.

THE HAPPINESS YOU SEEK WILL S

YOU MUST FIRST BECOME THE CHANGE YOU WANT TO SEE IN OTHER

MISSY AND DARREN
NEW YEARS EVE 2002

GOOD FORTUNE TO YOU THIS YEAR!

Good Fortune to You

I love to read my fortune more than I like to eat the fortune cookie. Sometimes I am extra lucky and get two! Fold your own fortunes up into paper fortune cookies. Allow each family member or friend to select a cookie. Scrapbook the fortunes along with a photo of each person.

Paper Lanterns

Light up your New Year! What looks like a complicated paper craft is actually very easy. Simply cut and fold to create these Chinese lanterns. Your fortunes can be hidden inside each or use them as a table decoration.

Happy New Year 2002!

A Bold Statement

A NEW YEAR'S TRADITION

This year, instead of making a resolution that you can only hope to keep, create a bold statement instead. I like to make them when I am about to start a big project. It helps me stay on course and to not get overwhelmed. Make your bold statement beautiful and hang it for everyone to see. You will be surprised how it will materialize before your very eyes.

Correspondence esta[...]

[...]re to which

[...]piness

the world can provide

My wishes for you... Love, Mom

You have everything

that you wish f[...]

New Year's Wishes

For my first New Year, my mother
wrote me a letter expressing all of her
wishes for me. I have taken excerpts
from the letter and made a beautiful
layout for my personal scrapbook.
I can feel her love and hope for
me each time I look at it.

Resolutions and Goals
For the New Year
2003

Resolution Album

I always want to be more thoughtful, have more time, have patience with others, and most of all be thankful for what I have. I put these thoughts and many others into a resolution album for this year. This is to keep me on track so I don't lose sight of what is important. Create an album like this for yourself as a gift to you!

Purse of Promises

This isn't just a scrapbook fashion accessory, it is a purse full of personal commitments. To find more time is my overall goal for the year. Time for family, friends, and to travel for pleasure instead of business. I can look back on this cute mini album next year and see how I did!

New Year's
TRADITIONS

CHAMPAGNE WISHES
A Toast

Materials

1 sheet of Gold Solid (AG029)
1 sheet of Gold Vellum (AG238)
1 sheet of Wheat Pattern (AG040)
2 sheets of Black Floral (AG059)
2 sheets of Gold Floral (AG107)
1 black frame (AG415)
Black card stock
Gold embossing powder
Heat tool
Ink pads: gold, white
Metal-edged vellum tags
Metal heart
Rubber stamps: heart, script
Silver card stock
Silver heart eyelet charm
Silver paper
Silver photo corners
Silver tags
Silver wire or champagne bottle wire
Stipple brush
Tiny word titles
Wire cutters or jeweler's pliers

Directions

Stipple gold ink onto black card stock, black frame, and edges of black floral paper. Allow to dry.

On black card stock and black frame, stamp script in white ink randomly over the frame. Cut an uneven heart shape and two small tags from the black card stock.

Shape a heart from the silver wire, using jeweler's pliers.

Cut 1" square from silver card stock. Ink with gold ink, then cover with embossing powder and heat. While that layer is still warm, add more embossing powder and reheat. Repeat again.

While embossing powder is still hot, press heart-shaped rubber stamp into it and remove carefully. This gives an impression like a wax seal.

Using foam adhesive, add irregular stamped heart, embossed heart, and wire heart to square tags. Add words and wire, also using foam adhesive.

Use pliers to twist and curl silver wire to connect the embellished tags. Add a silver heart eyelet charm to the wire also.

Add wired tags, then mat frame. Add journaling and photos with silver paper for a background and photo corners.

Treasured Moments

Directions

Cut black floral paper and black/gold pattern paper to 9"x12". Place, but do not adhere, the two sheets back-to-back. Fold 4" from the left and 2½" from the right to form the card.

To make the pop-up tabs, make small cuts horizontally across the inside folded sheet only. On the left side, make a ¾" cut across the fold at 1½" and 2½" from the top. On the right side, make a ¾" cut across the fold at 4" and 5" from the top.

Open the card and fold the tabs in. Attach the two sheets back-to-back with adhesive. Attach the die-cut flowers to the pop-up tabs.

Using the oval frame as a template, cut an oval from patterned paper. Set aside.

To make the ribbon-edged frame, cut 36" from ribbon. With one edge of the ribbon, pull the wire out slightly and bend to secure. With the opposite edge of the ribbon, pull the same wire that you have secured to gather the ribbon.

Apply adhesive to the back of the frame and shape the gathered ribbon around the frame. Insert the photo, then cover the back of the frame with patterned paper oval. Attach to front of gate-folded card.

Remove a small amount of wire from the roll, but keep it coiled. Use these coils to attach die-cuts to the second page, by taping one end to the paper or the die-cut.

Materials

1 sheet of Gold Pattern (AG027)
1 sheet of Gold Floral (AG107)
2 sheets of Black Floral (AG103)
2 sheets of Gold Solid (AG029)
3 sheets of Black/Gold Pattern (AG034)
1 die-cut (AG532)
4 die-cuts (AG522)
1 Oval Frame (AG428)
Gold craft wire
Green wire-edged taffeta ribbon

GOOD FORTUNE

Family Fortunes

Materials

1 sheet of Brown Solid (AG111)
1 sheet of Gold Floral (AG049)
1 sheet of Red Pattern (AG157)
2 sheets of Brown Pattern (AG110)
2 sheets of Gold Pattern (AG107)
4 sheets of Green Floral (AG116)
4 gold satin ribbon corners
1 die-cut (AG530)
Cream card stock

Circle cutter
Decorative scissors: deckle-edged,
  Victorian,
Red seam-binding ribbon

Directions

Cut an 11" circle from the red pattern paper. Adhere it onto gold floral paper and trim with decorative scissors, leaving a narrow border. Center and adhere circle onto page.

For the large fortune cookie, cut an 11" circle from the gold pattern paper. Fold in half. Fold again lightly at an angle and secure with foam squares for dimension. Adhere onto page.

Cut two sets of red flowers from a sheet of green floral paper. From the second sheet of the same paper, cut two sets of the large flowers only, and add to the bouquets of flowers with foam squares. Tie red ribbon around the stems. Adhere bouquets onto page.

Print fortunes on back of green floral paper. Cut them out, leaving the right end 1" longer than the fortunes. Roll the ends over ¼" and secure with adhesive.

For the small cookies, cut three 5" circles from gold pattern. Fold and add fortunes as before.

Good Fortune to You

Materials

1 sheet of Gold Pattern (AG107)
1 sheet of Gold Stripe (AG036)
1 sheet of Ivory Pattern (AG011)
1 sheet of Red Solid (AG028)
1 sheet of Red Stripe (AG095)
1 sheet of Wheat Pattern (AG040)
2 sheets of Red Pattern (AG002)
Rubber stamp: Chinese characters
Gold ink pad

Directions

To make fortune cookies, cut 4" circles from decorative papers. Use Good Fortune to You template on page 138. Glue two circles back-to-back. Print fortunes onto strips of ivory pattern paper. Lay one fortune on circle. Fold two sides of the circle up, overlapping edges slightly. Pull top and bottom edges of the circle together, leaving first fold on the outside edge of cookie. Adhere cookie together with foam tape.

Cut two 5"x12" pieces from wheat pattern paper and two from gold pattern.

Adhere them together back-to-back. These will become the flaps that open at the top and bottom of the page, so position the prints carefully.

Make the photo windows by measuring 1" in from each side and 1" in from the edge that will be in the center of the page. The windows are 3½" square.

Cut two 1"x12" strips from red stripe paper. Score along the length of the ribbon stripe to create a hinge piece.

Add hinge to flaps, one at the top and one at the bottom. Use these hinges to attach flaps to the background page.

Cut a 2"x12" strip from ivory pattern paper. Add to the center of the background of red pattern paper, so that it covers the gap between the flaps when closed. Place title banner here.

Stamp characters onto cream card stock in gold ink. Trim block for each character into a 2" square. Add fortunes and photos to page under flaps.

Materials
1 sheet of Gold Floral (AG049)
1 sheet of Red Stripe (AG095)
2 sheets of Gold Pattern (AG027)
2 sheets of Red Pattern (AG157)
Punch: bamboo

Directions
Fold a piece of red pattern paper in half. Use the Paper Lantern template on page 139 to make lanterns, matching up the folded edge. Cut the paper as indicated on the template. Unfold and mount onto page.

Use red stripes for fortunes to decorate and as lantern handles.

Use bamboo punch to create border on the red pattern paper and mount onto gold pattern paper.

Decoratively tuck photos and fortunes into the lanterns.

New Year's Wishes

Directions

Attach four 12" pieces of raffia around an 8" square of ivory paper and tie the edges. Mount onto the coral and green background papers. Add die-cut flowers onto the center. Insert envelopes into the die-cut flowers. Use the New Year's template on page 139 to make envelopes from ivory paper.

To create photo mats on second page, unroll raffia and adhere onto the back.

Materials
1 sheet of Blue Journal (AG245)
1 sheet of Green Floral (AG076)
1 sheet of Green Pattern (AG073)
2 sheets of Rose Floral (AG104)
3 sheets of Aqua Floral (AG058)
3 sheets of Aqua Pattern (AG055)
Cardboard
Decorative scissors: wide scallop
Green satin ribbon
Green satin ribbon corners

Materials
1 sheet of Aqua Pattern (AG055)
1 sheet of Blue/Green Pattern (AG158)
2 sheets of Blue Floral (AG147)
2 sheets of Green Pattern (AG003)
3 sheets of Coral Pattern (AG159)
1 die-cut (AG525)
1 die-cut (AG526)
Decorative scissors: scallop
Ivory paper
Raffia

Directions

Cut a 3" strip from aqua pattern paper with decorative scissors. Add a 2" strip of green pattern paper, then a 1½"-wide piece of satin ribbon. Attach to an 11" square of the green pattern paper. Using ribbon corners, attach square to the floral background.

To make the book cover, cut a 5"x15¼" strip of aqua pattern paper. To make the 15" strip, cut a 5"x8½" piece, and a 5"x7¾" piece. Overlap and adhere them together to make a 15¼"-long strip. Score ½" from each side and fold in.

Cut two 4¼"x7" pieces from cardboard. Adhere inside booklet cover, leaving a space in between to fold the spine. Adhere all sides onto cardboard.

Cut a 2"x5¼" strip from aqua pattern paper with decorative scissors. Attach a 1½" piece of green pattern paper to the front and then a ⅞"-wide piece of satin ribbon. Wrap the ribbon around the front cover and tie in a bow.

To make the inside of the book, cut the a left inside cover to 4"x7½" and a right inside cover to 4"x7" from the aqua pattern paper. Cut a scallop pocket.

Reverse the template and cut a pocket for the opposite side. Score, fold, and adhere onto the inside covers.

Insert resolution statement coupons inside booklet pockets.

Purse of Promises

Materials
1 sheet of Aqua Pattern (AG055)
1 sheet of Blue/Green Pattern (AG067)
1 sheet of Blue/Green Stripe (AG066)
1 sheet of Green Pattern (AG003)
2 sheets of Blue Floral (AG065)
2 Oval Frames (AG434)
4 green satin ribbon corners
Blue satin ribbon
Decorative scissors: wide scallop
Mother-of-pearl button

Directions

To make the purse, cut pieces from blue/green pattern paper, using the Purse of Promises template on page 139. Score on fold lines and assemble the body of the purse.

Cut the flap piece and top edges of the body piece with decorative scissors. Cut front and back pieces at the same time. Add the flap piece to the body of the purse. Using foam adhesive, attach the button and the bow.

Cut two 1"x9" strips of paper. Adhere them together, back-to-back. Score them at a 45-degree angle, so that the ends will fold down and leave a handle. Attach the ends of the handle to the back of the purse.

To make the pleated edges, cut four 1¼"x12" strips from green pattern paper. Score them at ½" and ¼" intervals. Fold along score lines to create box pleats. Mount pleated strips onto the back of a 5¼"x6" sheet.

To make the woven background, cut ½"x6" strips from decorative papers: eight from the floral, eight from the pattern paper. Place the strips on the background page and loosely weave by going over one strip and under the next strip, leaving ¾" between the strips. Assemble into a mini scrapbook album. Cut 3½"x 4½" cards to fit inside.

Paper-crafting Basics

BASIC MATERIALS

Basic materials used in this book include: Craft knife, cutting mat, metal ruler, pencil, double-sided tape, foam dots, hole punch, scissors, decorative-edged scissors, and an embossing stylus. You may have other tools that make these scrapbook pages easier to make—feel free to use them.

BASIC TECHNIQUES

Adhesives
There are a variety of wonderful adhesives for crafting available on the market. The projects in this book used double-sided tape and dimensional foam dots in various sizes. When creating scrapbook pages, be certain to use acid-free, archival-quality adhesives.

Decorative Papers
Decorative papers can be used alone or mixed together. Be creative—you can cut out flowers from printed papers and layer the cutouts with foam dots to add dimension to your pages.

Dovetail Ribbon Ends
Dovetailing ribbon ends is a decorative way to finish a bow or knotted ribbon. After tying the bow or knot, fold the ends of the ribbon in half horizontally. Trim folded ribbon at an angle, approximately 1" in from the end. Unfold the ends for the dovetail effect.

Mitering Corners
To miter corners is to join two strips of paper together at a right angle creating a 45-degree diagonal line at the corner of the two strips. Using a craft knife, cut through both pieces from the inside corner to the outside corner. Remove the excess of both strips.

Paper Punching
Paper punching is a great way to add intricate detail to scrapbook projects quickly and easily. Place the punch on a firm surface. Slide the paper in between the punch blades, then push the top down until the paper pops out. For best results, lubricate the punch with a piece of waxed paper. Punching through tin foil can help sharpen and clean your paper punch. To position a punch exactly, turn the punch over and align through the base of the punch.

Scoring and Creasing
Scoring paper and card stock makes it much easier to fold. To make crisp folds, you need a straightedge and an embossing stylus or bone folder. To score, place your paper or card stock on a table and position the straightedge where you want the fold to be. Score the line with a stylus. Fold the paper along the scored line.

Tying a Bow
Begin by creating a loop with the ribbon, hold it in your left hand with your thumb, with the loop facing the ceiling. With the shorter end in front, pointing toward your wrist, the long end of ribbon in back comes up and over your hand. Push a loop from the long end behind the first loop and through itself. Pull left- and right-side loops taut with respective index fingers and thumbs. Tighten the bow by pulling the streamers while pinching the center.

Tying a Square Knot
Wrap ribbon in place around card or project. Cross right streamer over left, push under left side, and pull up. Cross top streamer over bottom streamer. Push up through loop. Pull ends taut and trim the excess ribbon.

Tying a Threaded Knot
Punch two holes about ¼" apart in your paper. Place each ribbon end through a hole. From the back, take the right streamer and thread it up through the left hole. Again from the back, take the left streamer and thread it up through the right hole. Pull the ends taut and trim away the excess ribbon.

Using a Craft Knife
Use a craft knife for precision cutting on your scrapbook pages. Working on a cutting mat, hold the knife like a pencil and drag it toward you, following the edge of a metal ruler.
- Always cut toward your body to maintain control over the knife.
- A good, sharp blade is essential to keep edges neat, so you may need to change your blade frequently.
- Always keep knives and blades out of the reach of children.

Templates

Chocolate Cake

Cake

Page 30 (Enlarge 200%)

Chocolate Cake

Cake Slice

Page 30

(Enlarge 200%)

Strawberry Cake

Frosting

Page 31 (Enlarge 200%)

131

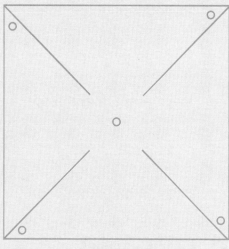

Pinwheels
Wishes

Pinwheel

Page 32 (Enlarge 400%)

Secret Wishes

Pink Envelope

Page 33 (Enlarge 200%)

Sweet
Sixteen

Envelope

Page 33 (Enlarge 200%)

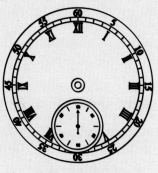

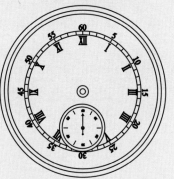

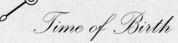

Time of Birth

Clock Faces & Hands

Page 34 (Full size)

Sisterly Love

Heart Weaving

(Half Weaving; Copy Twice)

Page 43 (Full size)

Easter Basket

Egg

Page 50 (Full size)

Easter Flowers

Flower Pot

Page 51 (Full size)

Easter Flowers

Flower Pot Rim

Page 51 (Full size)

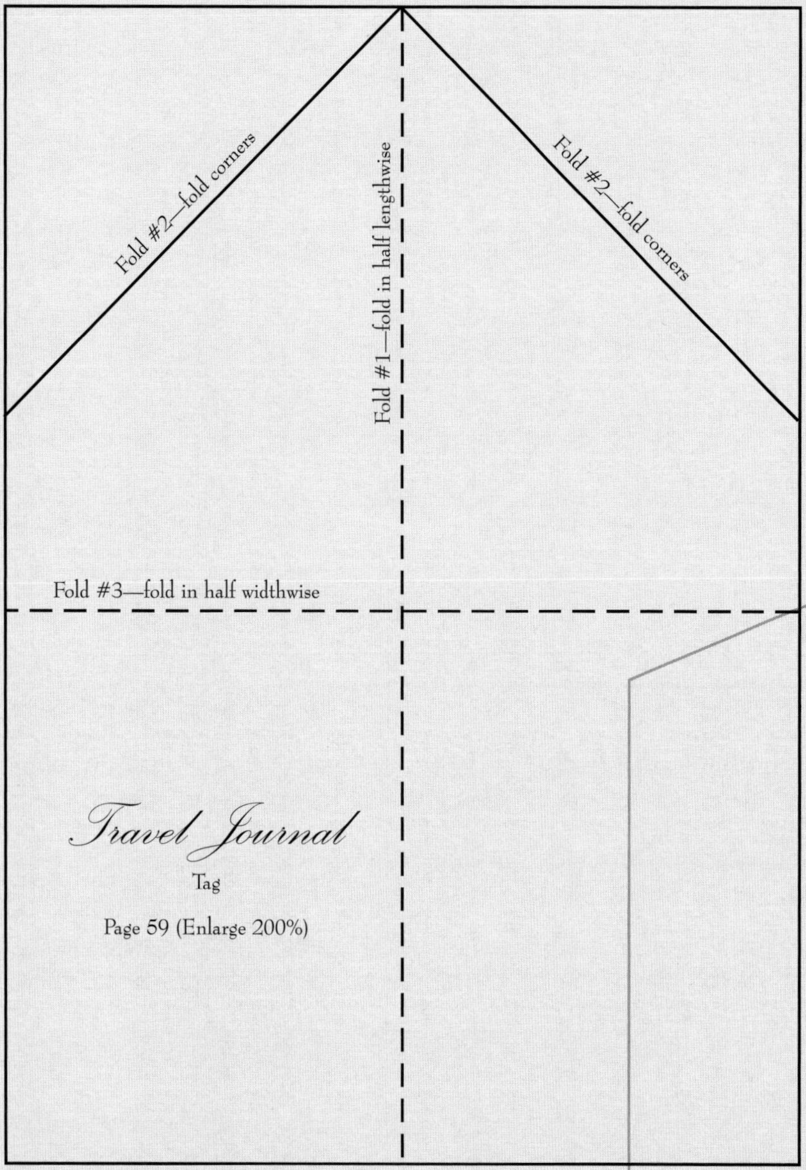

Fold #2—fold corners

Fold #1—fold in half lengthwise

Fold #2—fold corners

Fold #3—fold in half widthwise

Travel Journal

Tag

Page 59 (Enlarge 200%)

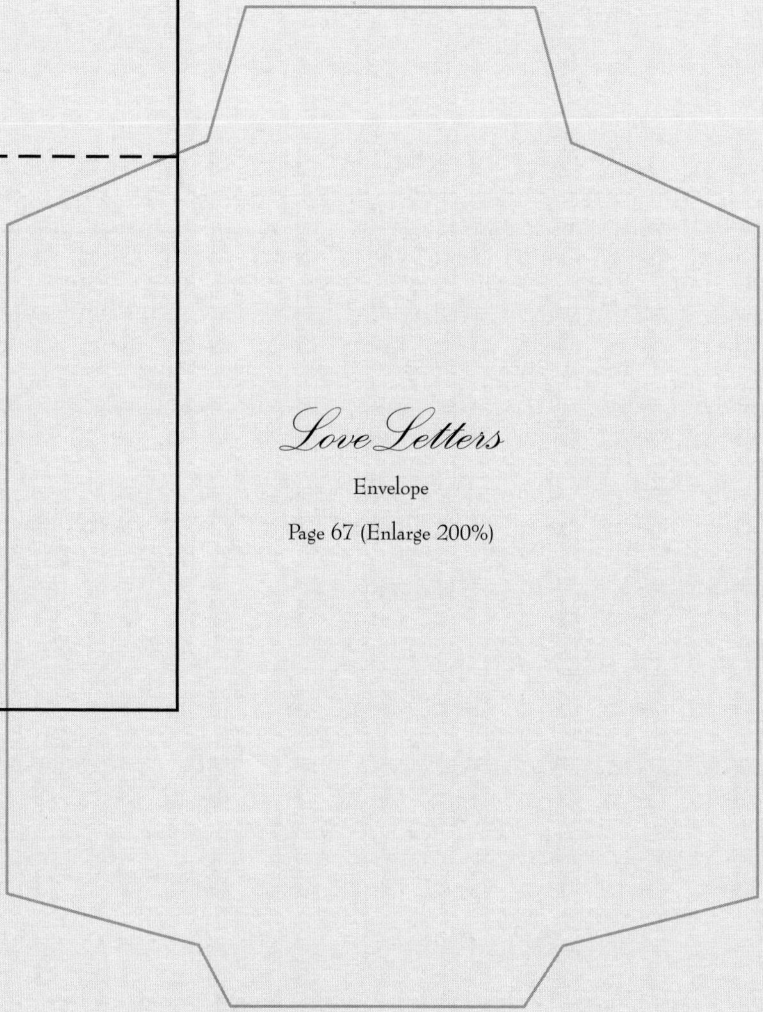

Love Letters

Envelope

Page 67 (Enlarge 200%)

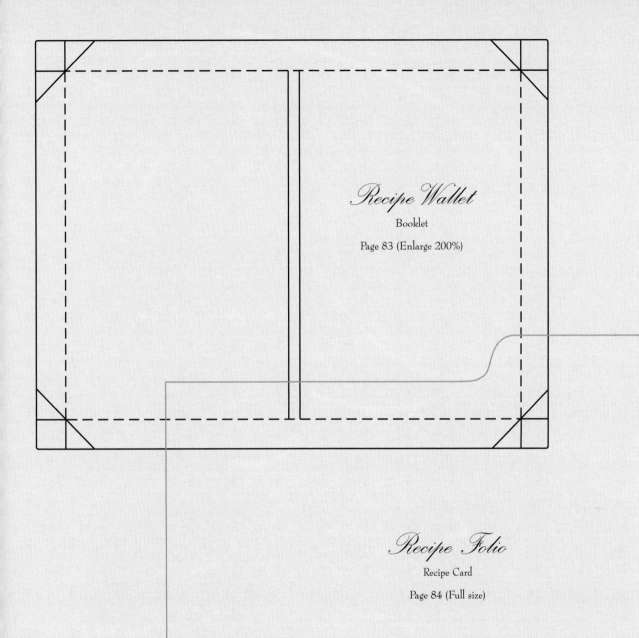

Recipe Wallet

Booklet

Page 83 (Enlarge 200%)

Recipe Folio

Recipe Card

Page 84 (Full size)

Mr. Turkey

Feather

Page 85 (Full size)

Christmas Kisses

Banner

Page 103 (Enlarge 150%)

Thanksgiving Headdress

Feather

Page 85 (Full size)

Christmas Kisses

Holly Leaf

Page 103 (Full Size)

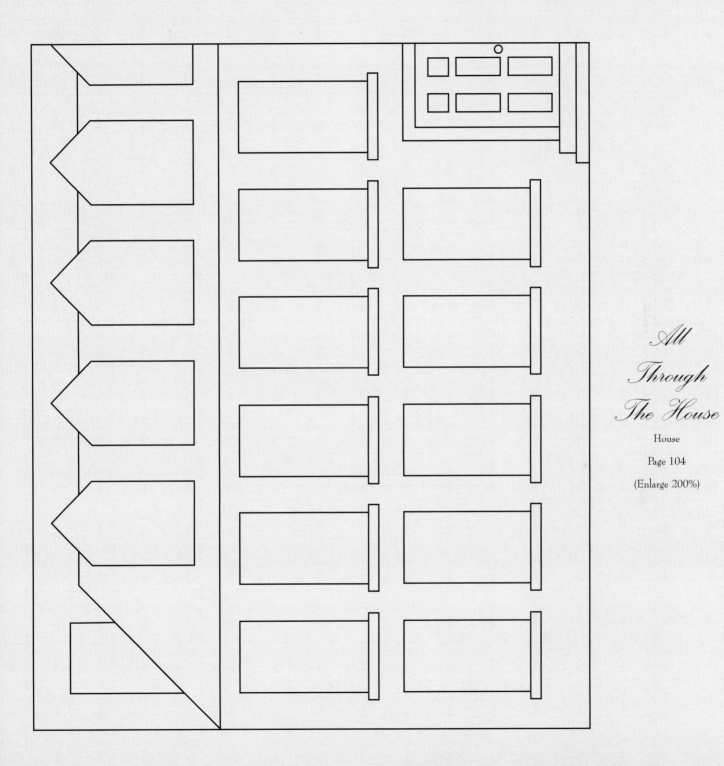

All

Through

the House

Windows

Page 104 (Full size)

Count to

Christmas

Envelope

Page 106 (Full size)

Good Fortune to You

Cookie

Page 126 (Full size)

Paper Lantern

Lantern

(Half Lantern; Copy Twice)

Page 127 (Full size)

Place fold here

New Year's Wishes

Wish Purse—body

Page 128 (Enlarge 200%)

139

Resources

Materials used in this book were manufactured by the following companies:

Anna Griffin, Inc.
733 Lambert Drive
Atlanta, GA 30324
888-817-8170
www.annagriffin.com

Artistic Wire
752 North Larch
Elmhurst, IL 60126
630-530-7536
www.artisticwire.com

Ellison Inc.
25862 Commercentre Drive
Lake Forest, CA 92630
800-253-2238
www.ellison.com

Fiskars Brands, Inc.
Fiskars School, Office & Craft
7811 West Stewart Avenue
Wausau, WI 54401
800-950-0203
www.crafts.fiskars.com

HERMAfix Adhesive
JM Technical Services
777 Terrace Avenue
Hasbrouck Heights, NJ 07604
888-236-8475

Jo-ann's Etc.
Customer Care
2361 Rosecrans Ave.
Suite 360
El Segundo, CA 90245
888-739-4120
www.joann.com

Kinko's
P.O. Box 1935
Provo, UT 84603-9926
www.kinkos.com
800-2-KINKOS

Kodak
Film & Digital Services
800-235-6325
www.kodak.com

Making Memories
1168 West 500 North
Centerville, UT 84014
800-286-5263
www.makingmemories.com

Martha Stewart
The Catalog for Living
800-950-7130
www.marthastewart.com

Michaels
8000 Bent Branch Dr.
Irving, TX 75063
800-MICHAELS
www.michaels.com

Office Depot
Corporate Support Center
2200 Old Germantown Road
Delray Beach, FL 33445
800-GO-DEPOT
www.officedepot.com

Offray Ribbon
Ninth Street & Bomboy Lane
Berwick, PA 18603
800-BERWICK
www.offray.com

Plaid Enterprises, Inc.
P.O. Box 7600
Norcross, GA 30091-7600
678-291-8100
www.plaidonline.com

Paper Style
11390 Old Roswell Road
Suite 122
Alpharetta, GA 30004
888-670-5300
www.paperstyle.com

Sam Flax
1460 Northside Drive
Atlanta, GA 30318
800-SAM-FLAX
www.samflax.com

3M
888-364-3577
www.3m.com

Glossary

A

Accordion Fold—A fold like the bellows of an accordion, folds forward then backward, in repeat.

B

Binding—The process of stitching or permanently adhering together a book.

C

Chalking—A technique of coloring or aging paper by rubbing with chalk.

D

Die-cut—To cut out around the edges of a print.

Dovetail—A notched end resembling a Dove's tail.

E

Embossing—The process of making designs or patterns in relief on paper.

Embossing Stylus—See *Stylus*

Eyelet—A small, metal fastener used to attach papers.

I

Ink Pad—Refers to ink used in rubber stamping with a thick consistency and rich color. Pigment inks will not dry on glossy surfaces.

J

Journaling—The written text on a scrapbook page.

M

Mat Board—A type of thick board, typically used for matting and framing photographs.

Miter—The edge of a piece of paper that has been beveled to meet with a smooth 45-degree joint.

Motif—A design or a thematic element.

P

Pleating—In paper crafting, to resemble a fold in cloth made by doubling material over on itself.

Q

Quill—To wind thread or yarn on a quill needle. To make a series of small rounded ridges in cloth.

R

Rubber Stamp—A stamp made of rubber used with an ink pad to make imprints and reproduce artwork.

S

Seam-binding Ribbon—A type of ribbon traditionally used in sewing.

Stylus—An instrument, usually with a pointed or ballpoint end, used for scoring or embossing paper.

T

Triangle—An instrument used to draw right angles.

V

Vellum—Translucent or semitranslucent paper or card stock.

W

Weaving—The process of forming a texture, fabric, or design by interlacing or intertwining elements.

Acknowledgments

Where would we be without those truly special people in our lives?

I know that I wouldn't be where I am without the strength and support of Tracey Flammer. I wouldn't look good or laugh without Holley Silirie. I wouldn't make my creative deadlines without Debby Schuh and Jenna Beegle, and I wouldn't be here at all if it were not for my wonderful parents, Sallie and Charles. Thank you all, from the bottom of my heart, for all you have given me!

Anna

Index